Activity Book

EXPLRING

GERMAN

Second Edition

Joan G. Sheeran

Consultants
Judy Gray Myrth
J. Patrick McCarthy

EMC Publishing, Saint Paul, Minnesota

ISBN 0-8219-1250-X

Published by EMC Publishing
300 York Avenue
St. Paul, Minnesota 55101

Printed in the United States of America
1 2 3 4 5 6 7 8 9 10 XXX 99 98 97 96 95

Unit 1

A Match column B with column A.

A		B
1. You say "hi" to a girl. _____		a. Wie heißt du?
2. You hope that your friend does _____ well at her music recital.		b. Tag, Renate.
		c. Es tut mir leid.
3. You ask a new student at school _____ what her name is.		d. Guten Abend.
		e. Tschüß, Gerhard.
4. You say "good-bye" to a friend. _____		f. Viel Glück.
5. You made a mistake and you _____ feel bad about it.		
6. You greet your neighbors as _____ they are leaving for an evening theater performance.		

B Name the language (in German) spoken in each country.

1. Rußland

   Ich spreche _____ .

2. Frankreich

   Ich spreche _____ .

3. England/die Vereinigten Staaten

   Ich spreche _____ .

4. Spanien

   Ich spreche _____ .

5. Italien

   Ich spreche _____ .

C Guess (in English) what other languages I speak!

1. arabisch _____

2. vietnamesisch _____

3. chinesisch _____

4. schwedisch _____

5. japanisch _____

D Introductions

Give this girl a German name.   Give this boy a German name.

_____   _____

Write their names in the spaces below and then complete the conversation.

(Girl's name) _____ : Tag! Wie heißt du?

(Boy's name) _____ : _____ .

(Girl's name) _____ : Ich heiße _____ .

(Boy's name) _____ : Es freut _____ .

(Girl's name) _____ : A_____ !

E Respond appropriately.

Beispiel (Example)   Andreas: Guten Tag, Herr Bach.
                         Herr Bach: Guten Tag, <u>Andreas</u>.

1. Patrick: Tag, Lars.

   Lars: _____ , Patrick.

2. Karl: Antje, sprichst du russisch?

   Antje: _____ , ich spreche russisch.

3. Christl: Sprichst du französisch?

   Holger: _____ , ich spreche nicht französisch.

4. Manfred: Wie heißt du?

   Lise: _____ heiße Lise.

5. Heinz: Wie geht's?

   Jutta: _____ , danke.

F Imagine that it's the first day of school. You and your partner play the roles of two students who haven't met yet. Carry on a short conversation in German in which each of you tries to find out as much information as you can about the other. Limit your questions to those you have already practiced in class and be sure to respond appropriately to your partner's questions or comments. For example, you might:

1) say "hello" or "hi" to your partner.
2) ask your partner what his or her name is.
3) ask your partner how he or she is.
4) ask your partner if he or she speaks French/Spanish/Italian/Russian.
5) tell your partner "good luck."
6) tell your partner "good-bye" and "see you later."

G Wörterrätsel

```
            I T A L I E N I S C H G X
            A E C X N F G E C I E L O T J
          Y K I B L N T F Z H P D B A A P D
          M N A F O S C E J N S F E X I S H N G
        N A L P Q U I S N E E P A C Y O T Ä U Z A
      W D A N G E N E H M N I R L E I D M T B E R M
      G I M I N J I O N S T L E T S T H E G E I W C
      L D E D Ö H S E H C P B C S A M N A S P S E R
      P U C H Y K O C R H C T H V U T I E Y K L D G
      K H T O E F S F E O K E E O A I L I I U I N M
      J G I L L I W Y S L U D R G Z T A C S N U V Q
      I O A R N H S A F X L K U K B E U T S G H I G
      D F S A T C Y S U I D U S B T Q I R I B H U R
      E R P E H S D O T G I C S P A E L D H R T I N
      Y S V X F I E I T D G S I H K C L O W E O W M
      J E R A A S U K O N U B S H D U W K N N C B Y
      K O L T D Ö T X C G U L C E H Y L M Z D D N N
      A H V F Z S I M S G I H C A M O F T A H Y
        T N G N C E N G L I S C H R D R E W T
          E O A H A Y F A T R I G D P V N R
            S R E E Ö D N R W E N D K O A
              F N H M E C H N I N A R M
```

1. WIE HEISST DU (SS=ß)	11. ANTJE
2. BITTE	12. HÖFLICHKEIT
3. JOSEF	13. GUTEN MORGEN
4. DANKE	14. GUTEN TAG
5. WIE GEHTS (apostrophe deleted)	15. SPANISCH
6. ENTSCHULDIGUNG	16. FRANZÖSISCH
7. JA	17. DEUTSCH
8. NEIN	18. ITALIENISCH
9. ANGENEHM	19. ENGLISCH
10. WILLI	20. ICH SPECHE RUSSISCH

H *Was weißt du?* (What do you know?) Look at the various announcements that appeared in German newspapers and identify the persons who are described. Here are some words that might be helpful to know: *wird...Jahre alt* (is...years old); *Papi* (Dad); *heute wirst Du...Jahr'* (today you'll be...years old); *Geburtstag* (birthday); *Herzliche Glückwünsche zur goldenen Hochzeit* (Congratulations on your golden wedding anniversary).

Guten Morgen

Hallo Tanja, 16 16

alles klar, heute wirst Du 16 Jahr'. Nun kannst Du auf die Pauke hau'n, und Dich so manches trau'n. Bis heute nachmittag!

Alles Gute von

Deiner Patentante nebst Anhang 16 16

Hallo MB 29
Alles Liebe zum
Geburtstag
wünscht Dir
Deine J 22

Hallo Hallo Hurra! 1 1
Nadinchen wird
heute schon 1 Jahr.
Viel Glück und Sonnenschein
das wünschen Dir
Oma und Opa 1 1

WILLI   LISA
Herzliche Glückwünsche zur goldenen Hochzeit
und weiterhin glückliche,
gemeinsame Lebensjahre.
Walgitta, Dieter, Jürgen, Dirk,
Michael und Angela
Lödingsen d. 14. 10.

Liebes Silberpaar in Nikolausberg
25 Jahre jetzt 'am Hut',
gesund, zufrieden, frohgemut.
Ein Grund zum Feiern, darum kommen am 15.10.
alle, das ist doch klar!!!
Bis bald grüßen
Aneliese u. Rudolf, Karin u. Dieter, Gertrud u. Manfred,
Bärbel u. Günter, Susanne u. Dietmar

Grüße + Glückwünsche

GLÜCKWÜNSCHE

HENNI PICKEL, Angerstein, Kirchstr. 4, feiert heute ihren 81. Geburtstag.
FRIEDRICH KAEGLER, Angerstein, Kirchstr. 15, wird heute 77 Jahre alt.
MINNA BUSSE, Erbsen, Mühlenweg 1, vollendet heute ihr 79. Lebensjahr.
ANNA DORSTEWITZ, Reiffenhausen, Am Heerberge 8, begeht heute ihren 86. Geburtstag.
KURT FISCHER, Dransfeld, wird am heutigen Donnerstag 79 Jahre alt.
BERTA AHLBORN, Dransfeld, feiert heute ihren 74. Geburtstag.
HANS KACKERT, Varmissen, begeht heute seinen 79. Geburtstag.

Guten Morgen, Papi!

50 *Jahre sind zerronnen, seit Du auf die Welt gekommen. Hast im Leben viel geschafft, brauchtest oft Geduld und Kraft. Du hast dafür gesorgt: ich hab' nichts entbehrt, und hast mir eine sorglose Kindheit beschert. Hast Dich gefreut, wenn ich gelacht und mich zu 'nem brauchbaren Menschen gemacht. Für all das Schöne, das Du mir gegeben, herzlichen Dank und*

„Hoch sollst Du leben!"
Alles Gute – Deine Mizzi
Mitgenfeld-Berlin, den 13. 10.

Wir gratulieren

Freitag, 15. Oktober

In Lohr Frau Philippine Bregenzer, Würzburger Straße 12, zum 79. Geburtstag; Frau Hedwig Lembach, Ruppertshüttener Straße 58, zum 75. Geburtstag.
In Steinfeld Frau Rosa Eder, Karl-Barthels-Straße 3, zum 76. Geburtstag; Herrn Hubert Dittrich, Am Hühnerberg 2, zum 71. Geburtstag.

This person...

1. lives in Dransfeld and is 79 years old today. _____

2. has a dad who is 50 years old. _____

3. is 16 years old today. _____

4. lives in Steinfeld, Karl-Barthels-Straße 3. _____

5. is one year old today. _____

6. will be 75 years old on October 15. _____

7. has been married to Willi for 50 years. _____

8. lives at Kirchstraße 4. _____

9. sends best wishes on a 25th wedding anniversary along with Bärbel, Günter, Gertrud, Manfred, Rudolf, Dietmar, Aneliese, Dieter and Susanne. _____

10. lives on the same street as Henni Pickel. _____

Unit 2

A   Answer *auf deutsch*.

1.   What can you use to make sure a line
     is straight?   _____

2.   What can you use to transfer your thoughts
     onto paper?   _____

3.   What can you wave at a parade?   _____

4.   What gives you a place to sit down?   _____

5.   In what can you draw pictures or keep notes?   _____

B   Answer the question by using the word in parentheses. *Auf deutsch, bitte.*

Was ist das?

1.   Das ist eine _____ . (wall)

2.   Das ist ein _____ . (classroom)

3.   Das ist ein _____ . (board eraser)

4.   Das ist eine _____ . (flag)

5.   Das ist ein _____ . (desk)

6.   Das ist eine _____ . (clock)

C How is each object used? Match column B with column A.

A		B
1. ein Buch _____		a. lets in fresh air and daylight
2. ein Fenster _____		b. gives you a place to throw used paper and trash
3. ein Bild _____		c. makes a plain room more attractive
4. ein Papierkorb _____		d. opens up new worlds of adventure, fantasy, travel and information
5. ein Spitzer _____		e. makes a dull point sharp

D List the items you have in your bookbag or pencil case. *Auf deutsch, bitte.*

_____

_____

_____

_____

_____

_____

_____

E Name the classroom object most closely associated with the following cues. *Auf deutsch, bitte.*

1. 9:00, 5:30 _____

2. Guatemala, Romania, China _____

3. *The Adventures of Huckleberry Finn, Moby Dick, Sleeping Beauty* _____

4. fresh air, shiny glass _____

5. storage for dictionaries, piece of furniture _____

6. separation of rooms, extension to ceiling _____

F Find your way through the classroom. Name the classroom objects you encounter on your way.

_____   _____

_____   _____

                                         _____

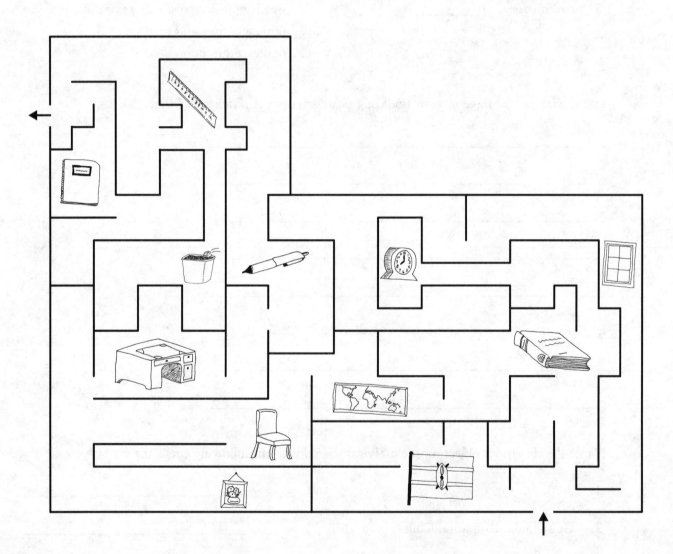

G Choose any ten classroom objects. As you point to each one, ask your partner what it is. Keep a record of how many objects your partner correctly identifies. Then reverse roles. This time you identify the objects your partner points out. See who can name the most items correctly.

Beispiel   You ask: Was ist das?

               Your partner answers: Das ist ein Buch.

Name: _____ Datum: _____

 Was weißt du? The following is a list of elementary schools in Göttingen, a city in northern Germany. Look at the list and answer the questions that follow. Here are some words you may need to know: *Schulverwaltungsamt* (school administration office); *Leiter/Leiterin, Rektor/Rektorin* (director or principal); *Grundschule* (elementary school).

Schulen

Schulverwaltungsamt
Neues Rathaus
Geismarlandstr. 4
geöffnet; montags bis freitags
8.30 - 12.00 Uhr, außerdem
donnerstags 14.00 - 17.00 Uhr
Leiter: Herr Geffers
☎ 4 00-24 95/24 96

Grundschulen

(Sprechstunden der Schulleiter
nach Vereinbarung)

Adolf-Reichwein-Schule
Göttingen-Geismar, Schulweg 14
☎ 4 00-51 19
Rektorin: Frau Radatz

Brüder-Grimm-Schule
Robert-Koch-Str. 11
☎ 4 00-47 11
Rektor: Herr Dr. Schipper

Egelsbergschule
Bebelstr. 25 ☎ 4 00-20 62
Rektorin: Frau Eichele

Erich-Kästner-Schule
Göttingen-Grone, Sollingstr. 1
☎ 4 00-56 40
Rektor: Herr Gande

Godehardschule
(kath. Grundschule)
Grätzelstr. 1 ☎ 4 00-53 47
Rektor: Herr Mondigler

Grundschule Elliehausen
Harrenacker 1 ☎ 4 00-54 30
Rektor: Herr Penkalla

Grundschule Herberhausen
Göttingen-Herberhausen
Eulenloch 6 ☎ 4 00-50 55
Schulleiterin: Frau Vehrenkamp

Hagenbergschule, Pappelweg 3
☎ 4 00-54 40
Rektor: Herr Lemke

Hainbundschule Weende
Göttingen-Weende
Ernst-Fahlbusch-Str. 22
☎ 4 00-52 40
Rektorin: Frau Weiland

Henneberg-Schule
Göttingen-Weende
Petrikirchstr. 21 ☎ 4 00-47 35
Rektor/in: N.N.

Herman-Nohl-Schule
Immanuel-Kant-Str. 44
☎ 4 00-28 74
Rektor: Herr Lutz

Höltyschule
Am Pfingstanger 38
☎ 4 00-50 41
Rektorin Frau Marten

Janusz-Korczak-Schule
3400 Göttingen-Nikolausberg
Auf der Lieth 1 ☎ 4 00-47 40
Schulleiter: Herr Hartung

Leinebergschule
Weserstr. 32 ☎ 4 00-56 50
Rektor: Herr Gebauer

---

1. The school administration office opens at 8:30 on Monday morning. When does it close?

   _____

2. What is the telephone number of the *Henneberg-Schule*?

   _____

3. Who is the principal of the *Godehardschule*?

   _____

4. On which street is the *Hagenbergschule* located?

   _____

5. What is the name of the school at which Mrs. Radatz is the principal?

   _____

6. What is the name of the school that has this telephone number: 4 00-52 40?

   _____

7. Is the principal at the *Erich-Kästner-Schule* a man or a woman?

   _____

8. How many elementary schools are there in Göttingen?

   _____

9. In which office does Mr. Geffers work?

   _____

10. Two of the principals, who have their offices in an elementary school building, have last names that start with the same first letter. What are their names?

   _____

Unit 3

 A *Wähle die richtige Antwort.* **Your friend wants you to do certain things. Which command does he or she give you to...**

1. say something in German?

    a. Sag das auf deutsch!

    b. Schreib auf deutsch!

2. read a note?

    a. Hör zu!

    b. Lies!

3. sit down?

    a. Sprich!

    b. Setz dich!

4. raise your hand?

    a. Geh an die Tafel!

    b. Heb die Hand!

5. close the book?

    a. Mach das Buch zu!

    b. Mach das Buch auf!

B For each command find the word in the list which is most closely associated.

eyes   hand   chair   mouth   feet   ear

1. Heb: _____

2. Sprich: _____

3. Geh: _____

4. Hör zu: _____

5. Setz dich: _____

C Ergänze die Sätze.

1. Sag das auf _____ ! (German)

2. Geh an die _____ ! (board)

3. Nimm Papier _____ ! (out)

4. Mach das Buch _____ ! (open up)

5. Beantworte die _____ ! (question)

D Imagine that you are Erich's teacher and that you want him to do the following things: (1) sit down, (2) take out the book, (3) open the book, (4) read from the book, (5) close the book, and finally (6) go to the board. Number the following commands in the sequential order described.

_____ Lies das Buch!

_____ Setz dich!

_____ Geh an die Tafel!

_____ Mach das Buch auf!

_____ Nimm das Buch heraus!

_____ Mach das Buch zu!

E Write a command suggested by the word cue at the left.

1. Kuli, Bleistift _____

2. Buch _____

3. Musik (*guess!*) _____

4. Stuhl _____

F Kreuzworträtsel

Vertical

2. Raise your hand.
3. "Ergänze die...."
4. to raise, lift
5. Speak.
8. commands
11. Write.
14. Say.
16. "...Buch" *(a)*

Horizontal

1. Open your book.
6. "...die Frage."
7. no
9. "...dich." (*Sit down.*)
10. "...zu." (*Listen.*)
12. "Nimm...heraus."
13. what Hänschen becomes
15. "Sag das auf...."
17. "Geh an die...."
18. "...jeden Satz." (*Complete each sentence.*)

Name: _____ Datum: _____

G With a classmate play *Simon sagt,* the German version of "Simon says." First give your partner a command. If you say *"Simon sagt"* before the command, your partner should perform the action ordered. If you do not say *"Simon sagt,"* however, your partner should ignore your command. Keep giving orders until your partner either performs incorrectly or makes a motion when you have not said *"Simon sagt."* Then it's your partner's turn to give orders. Perform your partner's commands until you slip up. See who can respond correctly to the most orders.

H *Was weißt du?* Imagine you are entering a classroom in Germany where students are learning English. On the wall you see student instructions that students follow every day. Can you figure them out? Write the appropriate number after each equivalent expression in English.

Unsere Klassenregeln

1. Sprich immer laut und deutlich!
2. Mach die Fenster auf, wenn es warm ist!
3. Setz dich, wenn es klingelt!
4. Heb deine Hand, sobald du die Antwort weißt!
5. Nimm ein Blatt Papier heraus, wenn du schreiben mußt!
6. Hör immer gut zu!
7. Mach deine Bücher zu, wenn es eine Arbeit gibt!
8. Lies, was an der Tafel steht!
9. Schreib deinen Namen in dein Heft!
10. Sprich nicht, wenn der Lehrer spricht!
11. Geh nach der Schule sofort nach Hause!
12. Sag alles auf englisch!

---

a. Write your name in your notebook! _____
b. Always listen well! _____
c. Open the windows when it's warm! _____
d. Say everything in English! _____
e. Take out a sheet of paper when you have to write! _____
f. Don't speak when the teacher is speaking! _____
g. Always speak loudly and clearly! _____
h. Read what is on the board! _____
i. Go home immediately after school! _____
j. Close your books when there is a test! _____
k. Raise your hand as soon as you know the answer! _____
l. Sit down when the bell rings! _____

Unit 4

A   **Complete the missing numbers.**

1.   vierzig, _____ , sechzig

2.   zwanzig, _____ , achtzehn

3.   sechs, _____ , acht

4.   fünfzehn, _____ , fünf

5.   siebzig, _____ , neunzig

6.   zweiunddreißig, _____ , dreißig

B   **Match the word in column B with the Arabic numeral in column A.**

A	B
1. 2 _____	a. dreizehn
2. 8 _____	b. fünf
3. 13 _____	c. einundzwanzig
4. 5 _____	d. zwei
5. 21 _____	e. acht

C   **Numbers in Nursery Rhymes and Fairy Tales**

1.   How many lambs did Mary have?

     a.   eins   b.   elf

2.   How many little pigs were there?

     a.   sechs   b.   drei

3.   How many dwarfs did Snow White meet?

     a.   sieben   b.   neun

4.   How many stepsisters did Cinderella have?

     a.   zwei   b.   zwölf

5.   How many blackbirds were baked in the pie?

     a.   dreiundzwanzig   b.   vierundzwanzig

D   Numbers and Facts. *Wähle die richtige Antwort!*

1. How many planets are there?

   a. fünf   b. neun

2. How many toes does a person have?

   a. zehn   b. acht

3. How many feet does a duck have?

   a. zwei   b. vier

4. How many antlers does a reindeer have?

   a. eins   b. zwei

5. How many weeks make up a year?

   a. sieben   b. zweiundfünfzig

6. How many letters are there in the English alphabet?

   a. sechsundzwanzig   b. zwanzig

7. How many days are there in the month of November?

   a. einunddreißig   b. dreißig

8. How many items are in a dozen?

   a. dreizehn   b. zwölf

9. How many minutes make up three-quarters of an hour?

   a. fünfzehn   b. fünfundvierzig

10. How many candles will be on a child's eighth birthday?

    a. elf   b. acht

E *Wieviel kostet...?* Imagine that you are in a German supermarket and your host family, with whom you are living, has given you a shopping list. Figure out how much the items cost and come up with a total amount. If you get 50 marks, how much money will you bring back?

4 rolls (each roll costs .40 mark) _____

1/2 lb. butter (1 lb. costs 4.50 marks) _____

3 lbs. pork (1 lb. costs 5.20 marks) _____

2 liters milk (1 liter costs 1.70 marks) _____

1/4 lb. Swiss cheese (1 lb. costs 12.80 marks) _____

6 bananas (1 banana costs .60 mark) _____

TOTAL _____

RETURN _____

F *Schreib die Wörter richtig.* Unscramble the words.

1. HZEHAL _____

2. WELVIIE _____

3. FFNÜ _____

4. GERWEIN _____

5. FEL _____

6. ZUNIENG _____

7. NDU _____

8. HTACZNEH _____

9. ALM _____

10. NISE _____

G Draw:

1. "vier" cookies.

2. "sieben" happy faces.

3. "drei" trees.

4. "sechs" flowers.

5. "zwei" houses.

H *Wie viele Objekte gibt es hier?* **How many items are pictured? Circle the correct number.**

1. 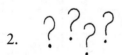 zwölf zehn dreizehn

2. sechzehn vier neun

3.  fünfzehn sieben drei

4.  eins elf zwei

5.  acht zwanzig drei

Name: _____ Datum: _____

I With your classmates play *Summ!* This game is similar to the English game "Buzz." Pick a number lower than 10, for instance, 7. To begin, all students must stand up. Each student counts off in German, starting with *null*. When the number 7, a number containing 7 or a multiple of 7 comes up, the student whose turn it is must say "*Summ!*" instead of the number. (For example, between 0 and 30 students should say "*Summ!*" instead of 7, 14, 17, 21, 27 and 28.) A student who responds incorrectly must sit down. The count picks up after the next student in line corrects the error by saying "*Summ!*" or the right number, depending on the type of mistake made. The winner of the game is the last person to remain standing.

J *Was weißt du?* Take a look at the chart and then fill in the blanks with the appropriate information. You will need to know the following words: *Stadt* (city); *Flughafen* (airport); *Entfernung zur Stadtmitte* (distance to downtown); *Kosten in Mark* (cost in marks); *Bahn* (train); *Fahrtzeit (min)* (driving time [minimum]); *km* (kilometer[s]).

Stadt	Flughafen	Entfernung zur Stadtmitte	Kosten in Mark			Fahrtzeit (min)		
			Taxi	Bus	Bahn	Taxi	Bus	Bahn
Amsterdam	Schiphol	15 km	54	—	4,70	30	—	25
Barcelona	Barcelona	15 km	30	5,60	3,50	60	30	20
Berlin	Tegel	8 km	40	3,20	—	40	30	—
Bonn	Köln/Bonn	28 km	60	7,00	—	40	36	—
Brüssel	National	12 km	45	—	3,80	20	—	20
Düsseldorf	Rhein-Ruhr	9 km	25	2,60	2,60	35	20	12
Frankfurt	**Rhein-Main**	**10 km**	**30**	**—**	**3,90**	**30**	**—**	**12**
Genf	Genève	4 km	33	- -	4,50	25	—	7
Hamburg	Fuhlsbüttel	15 km	25	3,40	—	40	24	—
Hannover	Langenhagen	11 km	30	4,90	2,90	30	20	45
Köln	Köln/Bonn	18 km	45	7,00	—	25	20	—
Leipzig	Leipzig	18 km	30	4,00	—	30	30	—
London	Heathrow	24 km	70	13,00	9,30	90	75	45
München	F. J. Strauß	35 km	85	12,00	10,00	60	45	40
Nürnberg	Nürnberg	6 km	20	4,50	—	30	19	—
Paris	Charles de Gaulle	23 km	67	15,00	7,00	60	55	55
Rom	Leonardo da Vinci	35 km	75	—	7,00	75	—	30
Stockholm	Arlanda	41 km	115	—	12,00	60	—	60
Stuttgart	International	13 km	40	6,00	4,00	30	23	27
Wien	Schwechat	18 km	50	8,60	4,30	25	20	35
Zürich	Kloten	12 km	50	—	4,90	30	—	15

1. It's _____ kilometers from Charles de Gaulle Airport to the center of Paris.

2. It costs _____ marks to take the bus from the airport in Leipzig to downtown.

3. It takes _____ minutes by taxi from the Stuttgart International Airport to the center of the city.

4. The airport in Hamburg is located in the suburb called _____ .

5. The train from the Rhein-Main Airport takes only _____ minutes to go to the main station in Frankfurt.

6. The farthest distance between the airport and the center of the city is when travelers land in _____ .

7. The distance between the airport and downtown is the shortest in the city of _____ .

8. The airport for Bonn also is used by people who live in the city of _____ .

9. The least expensive bus ticket to downtown of one of the listed cities costs _____ marks.

10. The most expensive cost either by taxi, bus or train is _____ marks.

Unit 5

A For what is each city famous? Match column B with column A.

	A			B
1.	Leipzig	_____	a.	Gothic cathedral
2.	Dresden	_____	b.	porcelain
3.	Berlin	_____	c.	Gewandhaus Orchestra
4.	München	_____	d.	Brandenburg Gate
5.	Köln	_____	e.	Oktoberfest

B Complete the following names of well-known items, places and events and then identify what each one is.

1. *Dresdner* _____ :

   _____

2. *4711 Kölnisch* _____ :

   _____

3. Spanish Riding _____ :

   _____

4. Pergamon _____ :

   _____

5. "Sound of _____ " :

   _____

6. *Leipziger* _____ :

   _____

Name: _____ Datum: _____

 C After studying the map in your textbook and reading the information on pages 27 and 28, answer the following questions. Circle the correct response.

1. Which city is fairly close to salt water (the sea)?

   Genf   Wien   Hamburg

2. Which city might attract a conference for international bankers?

   Zürich   Köln   Salzburg

3. Which city has a world-famous boys' choir?

   Wien   München   Bonn

4. Which city hosts a yearly parade at carnival time?

   Köln   Berlin   Bern

5. Which city is very close to a salt mine?

   Leipzig   Genf   Salzburg

D Study the map in your textbook as you identify the direction you travel from one city to another. Use these codes:

N = north   E = east   NE = northeast   NW = northwest
S = south   W = west   SE = southeast   SW = southwest

	FROM	TO	DIRECTION?
1.	München	Hamburg	_____
2.	Berlin	Dresden	_____
3.	Wien	Salzburg	_____
4.	Salzburg	Köln	_____
5.	Bern	Leipzig	_____
6.	Zürich	Genf	_____

E Using the map on page 27 of your textbook, draw Germany. Include cities and rivers.

F *Wörterrätsel.* Can you find 3 countries, 11 cities, 2 mountain ranges, 2 rivers and 2 seas?

```
Ö X N D O N A U B E M M O I Q J
V S O T A S I W A N E P L A D H
E I T I C A Z K U D E O S I Z W
L N Q E B J B C M I A S R M I L
R O B O R I X Ü I T W A F E B D
F D E A J R N Q S K Ö L N H O E
N I R J D C E S T G A Z J I N U
O P L E H R Y I L F S B E R N T
A R I E S A W M C O E U L V W S
X G N O R D S E E H T R U D K C
H S B I F L E I P Z I G Y O J H
Y R K P H O N N C Ü T S A S F L
G S T A A D B D X R N I M T L A
C Z O Q R R B L F I H C D S T N
U D Z W Z I E W H C S A U E S D
H D E T I B A K I H O R H E I N
```

G Imagine that you go to a travel agency to inquire about a trip to Germany. Your partner plays the role of the travel agent. Ask the agent about what cities you should visit and what you should see while you're there. Depending on your interests, plan your itinerary with the travel agent for a two-week trip. Then reverse roles so that your partner is the traveler. Come up with a different itinerary to fit your partner's interests.

Was weißt du? Imagine you and your classmates are in Frankfurt, Germany, and have just gone to the Tourist Information Office in the *Hauptbahnhof* (main station) to pick up a city map. Everyone has a different idea where to go in the city. Since you have the map, they all ask you how to get to certain places. Assume that everyone will start from the main station (see the "X" on the map). You're also lucky. You can give your directions in English as all the tourists speak the language. Give the tourists appropriate directions and tell them how to get to the indicated places.

Name: _____ Datum: _____

1. *Theaterplatz*

   _____

   _____

   _____

2. *Main* (River)

   _____

   _____

   _____

3. *Alte Oper*

   _____

   _____

   _____

4. *Römer*

   _____

   _____

   _____

5. *Festhalle/Messegelände*

   _____

   _____

   _____

6. *Schweizer Platz in Sachsenhausen*

   _____

   _____

   _____

7. *Palmengarten*

   _____

   _____

   _____

8. *Hauptwache*

   _____

   _____

   _____

Unit 6

A Match column B with column A.

A		B
1. Das Haus hat _____		a. in deiner Wohnung
2. Der Garten ist _____		b. Mietshaus
3. Wie viele Zimmer gibt es _____		c. schön
4. Hier ist _____		d. hinter dem Garten
5. Familie Schubert wohnt _____ in einem		e. sieben Zimmer
6. Die Garagen sind _____		f. mein Haus

B Draw a diagram or layout of your house or apartment. Label the rooms *auf deutsch*.

C   What would you most likely find in a *Wohnzimmer*? Circle the appropriate items.

Wand	Stück	Bücherschrank	Garage	Haus
Garten	Klassenzimmer	Kreide	Stuhl	Uhr
Zimmer	Fenster	Tafel	Mäuse	Bild

D   Where could you find...? Circle the appropriate words.

1. Zelt:

   in der Nordsee   in einer Villa   in den Alpen

2. Mietshaus:

   in einer Stadt   in einer Wohnung   in einem Garten

3. Eßzimmer:

   in einer Garage   in einer Küche   in einem Haus

4. Wohnwagen:

   in einem Garten   in einem Zelt   in einem Schlafzimmer

5. Badezimmer:

   in einem Einfamilienhaus   in einem Wohnzimmer   in einer Garage

Imagine that you've just moved into a new house. Your friend comes to visit and would like a tour. He or she asks you where each room is. For example, your friend says *"Wo ist die Küche?"* You point out the kitchen and say *"Hier ist die Küche."* Your friend asks you the location of the following rooms: *das Schlafzimmer, das W.C., das Wohnzimmer, das Badezimmer, die Küche, das Eßzimmer.*

He or she may also ask about the garage and the yard (*die Garage, der Garten*). After you point out all the locations, reverse roles. This time you ask where these places are and your friend points them out.

F *Was weißt du?* The following ads appeared in the *Frankfurter Rundschau*, a daily newspaper published in Frankfurt, Germany. The ads deal with the topic *Vermietungen Wohnungen —1 ½- und 2-Zimmer-Wohnungen* (Apartments for Rent — 1 ½- and 2-Room Apartments). The 12 apartments advertised are located in Frankfurt as well as in other towns and cities. In reading the description, can you figure out where these apartments are located? Here are some words and abbreviations that might help you in your answers: *Bad/Bäder* (bathroom/bathrooms); *Balkon* (balcony); *m²* (square meter[s]); *Einkaufszentrum* (shopping center); *in neuem Haus* (in a new house); *Keller* (basement); *Fußgängerzone* (pedestrian zone); *Kamin* (fireplace); *Schwimmbad* (swimming pool).

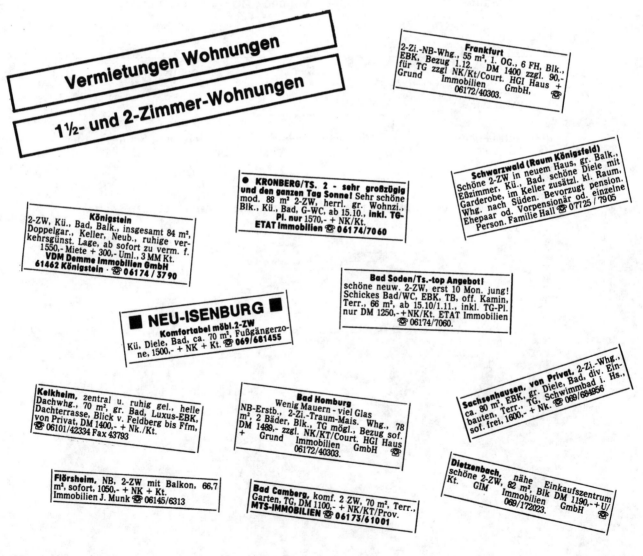

This apartment...

1. has a lot of glass and two bathrooms. _____

2. has a balcony and rents for 1,050 marks a month. _____

3. has a fax number if you want to find out more about it. _____

4. is the largest listed and is available after October 15. _____

5. is located near a shopping center. _____

6. is the smallest listed and is available after December 1. _____

7. has a basement and is located in a new house. _____

8. is located in a building along or near a pedestrian or walking zone. _____

9. has a garden and is 70 square meters in size. _____

10. has a fireplace and rents for 1,250 marks a month. _____

11. can be inquired about by calling 06174/3790. _____

12. has access to a swimming pool. _____

G Find your way back to your bed. Name each type of house or shelter you find along the way.

_____

_____

_____

_____

_____

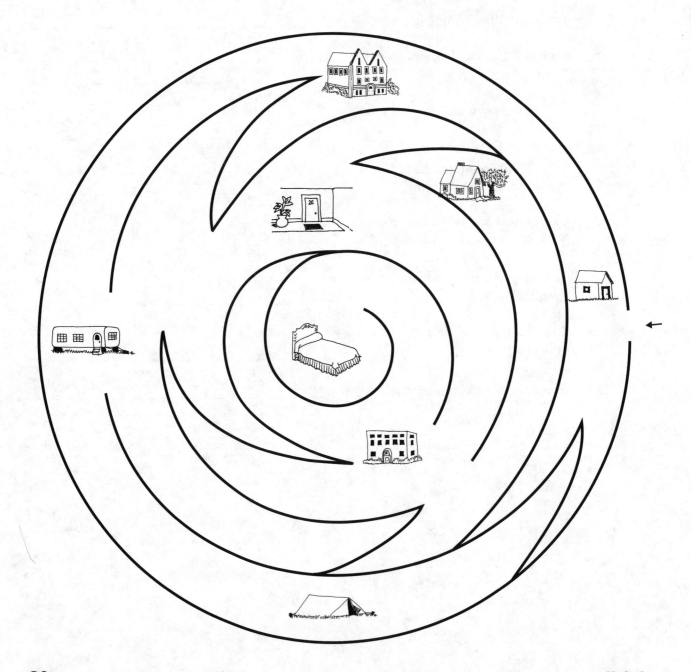

Unit 7

A Write the first and last name (if different from yours) of each family member listed.

1. Mutter

   _____

2. Vater

   _____

3. Bruder

   _____

   _____

   _____

4. Schwester

   _____

   _____

   _____

5. Tante

   _____

   _____

   _____

6. Onkel

   _____

   _____

   _____

7. Großvater (mother's side)

   _____

8. Großmutter (mother's side)

   _____

9. Großvater (father's side)

   _____

10. Großmutter (father's side)

   _____

B Make your own family tree by labeling each person's name and his or her relationship to you. Start at the bottom by labeling your name and the names of any brothers or sisters. Next, show your parents, their siblings, parents, etc.

C Circle the person who does not fit in with the rest.

1. Nichte	Tante	Neffe
2. Großvater	Schwester	Bruder
3. Mutter	Cousin	Frau
4. Enkelin	Großmutter	Sohn
5. Pate	Onkel	Tochter
6. Vater	Kusine	Mann

D Circle *ja* or *nein*.

1. Hast du (*Do you have*) Paten?   ja   nein
   Wenn „ja" *(if "yes")*, wie heißen sie? _____

2. Hast du einen Cousin?   ja   nein
   Wenn „ja", wie heißt er? _____

3. Hast du eine Tante?   ja   nein
   Wenn „ja", wie heißt sie? _____

4. Hast du eine Schwester?   ja   nein
   Wenn „ja", wie heißt sie? _____

5. Hast du einen Bruder?   ja   nein
   Wenn „ja", wie heißt er? _____

E Identify each relative or family member and write down the German name.

1. A man who has a son or daughter. _____

2. A female child who is related to a mother and father. _____

3. A son of one's brother or sister or one's brother-in-law or sister-in-law. _____

4. Mother's or father's brother. _____

5. The mother of one's father or mother. _____

6. The female who has a brother. _____

7. A female child of one's uncle or aunt. _____

8. A male who has the same parents as another or one parent in common with another. _____

F Bring to class a family photo showing as many of your relatives as possible. (If you can't find a photo, you may draw a picture of your relatives. You might choose to bring a picture of your imaginary family from the back issue of a magazine or newspaper.) Your partner will ask you who each person is. After you answer, your partner will ask you the name of each person.

Beispiel	Your partner asks:	Wer ist das?
	You answer:	Das ist meine Tante.
	Your partner asks:	Wie heißt sie?
	You answer:	Sie heißt Katrin.

Then reverse roles. This time you ask about your partner's family members.

G *Was weißt du?* Family announcements for various happy and sad occasions are published in every major German newspaper. Find the ad that matches each description. Write the letter of the ad following each description. These words may be helpful for you to know: *Oma und Opa* (grandma and grandpa); *Jahr'/Jahre* (years); *alle Verwandten und Bekannten* (all relatives and friends); *Geburtstag* (birthday); *Schwiegereltern* (parents-in-law); *um elf Uhr* (at eleven o'clock); *Verlobung* (engagement); *die letzten Wochen* (the last weeks); *glücklich* (happy).

a
Hopp(e), hopp(e), hopp(e)
Ulli
läuft Galopp
Es ist sein größter Wille – Katja heißt bald Hille.
Um elf Uhr sagen sie endlich ja
und abends kommt die ganze Schar

b
Unserer lieben Mutti, Oma und Uroma
Elisabeth
alle guten Wünsche
zum **83.** Geburtstag.
Alle Verwandten und Bekannten

d
Liebes Krümel
zu Deinem 35. Geburtstag
wünsche ich Dir alles Liebe.
Ich liebe und brauche Dich.
Dein Frettchen und Baron

e
Liebe Tinamaus
Zur Verlobung die besten
Glückwünsche.
In Liebe
Dein Zockelbär

c
In stiller Trauer nehmen wir Abschied von meinem lieben Mann, Vater, Schwiegervater, Opa und Uropa
Werner Aßmann
geb. 13. März 1912
gest. 30. Sept. 1993
In Liebe:
Charlotte Aßmann im Namen aller Angehörigen

f
Mein lieber, kleiner „Kacker"!
Die letzten Wochen waren wunderschön! Ich bin wahnsinnig glücklich mit Dir!
In Liebe, Deine „Püppi"

g
Oma Marianne!
Du machst den anderen so viel Freude durch Deine liebevolle Art, deshalb danken wir Dir heute. Viel Glück und einen wunderschönen Tag.
Herzlichen Glückwunsch zum Geburtstag.
Dieter, Andreas, Sandra, Thomas, Ute, Jan Patrick.

i
Liebe Eltern u. Schwiegereltern!
50 Jahre seid Ihr nun vereint, das Leben hat es nicht immer nur gut mit Euch gemeint, habt manchen Sturm erlebt, auch die Wände sind manchmal erbebt, trotz allem habt Ihr zusammengehalten, um Eure Ehejahre glücklich zu gestalten. Viel Glück u. Gesundheit für die kommenden Jahre wünschen Euch
Wolfgang, Gudrun, Thorsten, Mario, Anke, Sven und Corinna

J
Wie schön, daß Du geboren bist, wir hätten Dich sonst sehr vermißt. Es war einmal vor 10 Jahr', da rief die Sabrina, Papa, ich bin da.
Drum wünschen wir von Herzen alles Gute
Oma und Opa

h
Wir vermissen Dich sehr!
Ein aufopfervolles und von Liebe zu ihren Kindern und Enkeln geprägtes Leben ging viel zu früh zu Ende.
Lisa Kaufmann
geb. Schulze
geb. 30. Aug. 1927   verst. 31. Aug. 1993
Wir nehmen Abschied in Liebe und Dankbarkeit:
**Deine Töchter Evi und Kerstin
Deine Enkel Nadine und Nico
sowie Jürgen und Lothar**
Die Urnenfeier findet am Freitag, dem 15. Oktober 1993, 13.00 Uhr auf dem Friedhof Wahren statt.

In this announcement...

1. the grandmother and grandfather congratulate their granddaughter on her tenth birthday. _____

2. all relatives and friends send her their best wishes on her birthday. _____

3. the children and grandchildren mourn the death of this 66-year-old woman. _____

4. Thomas and five other grandchildren congratulate their grandmother on her birthday. _____

5. seven people wish their parents and parents-in-law well on their 50th wedding anniversary. _____

6. friends inform everyone that Katja will get married at eleven o'clock. _____

7. best wishes for an engagement are announced. _____

8. a woman tells how happy she has been with her boyfriend or husband during the last few weeks. _____

9. the death of an 81-year-old man is announced. _____

10. this person congratulates his spouse on her 35th birthday. _____

H Kreuzworträtsel

Vertical

1. boy's name
2. godparents
3. nephew
5. niece
7. children
8. brother
10. girl's name
11. daughter of Josef and Judith
13. parents' female child
15. parents' male child
17. "eins und zwei =..."

Horizontal

1. "...ist das?"
2. godmother
4. granddaughter
6. grandchildren
9. family
12. parents
14. mother
16. "...Kind"
18. male parent
19. another daughter of Judith and Josef
20. "Wie heißt...Junge?"

Unit 8

A

Certain occupations require special skills. Match the talent or skill to the job.

A		B
1. Mechanikerin _____		a. has good sense of rhythm
2. Koch _____		b. knows how and when to plant crops
3. Elektrikerin _____		c. can help keep you healthy
4. Tischler _____		d. has good sense of color and perspective
5. Ärztin _____		e. knows how to fix an engine
6. Schauspieler _____		f. can create appetizing delicacies
7. Musikerin _____		g. imitates well and memorizes early
8. Klempner _____		h. knows hard wood from soft wood
9. Landwirtin _____		i. knows how to bring light into a house
10. Künstler _____		j. can repair a leaking faucet

B

Name the people needed to:

1. build a house.

   _____   _____

   _____

2. take care of your health.

   _____   _____

3. entertain you in the theater and the concert hall.

   _____   _____

4. keep you in contact with your pen pal in Austria.

   _____

5. instruct you about civilization, the arts and the sciences.

   _____

Choose the subject area most closely associated with each occupation.

1. Arzt

   a. science   b. music   c. agriculture

2. Musikerin

   a. geography   b. fashion   c. orchestra

3. Landwirt

   a. art   b. botany   c. literature

4. Geschäftsfrau

   a. drama   b. automotive engineering   c. marketing

5. Koch

   a. nutrition   b. history   c. math

6. Künstlerin

   a. construction   b. painting   c. medicine

D **Complete the sentences.**

1. Was ist dein Beruf? Ich _____ Lehrer.

2. Was _____ du? Ich bin Köchin.

3. Hoffmanns Arbeitsvermittlung _____ Mechaniker.

4. Der Künstler _____ in einer Villa.

5. Frau Polinski _____ einen Beruf.

6. Jeder _____ seines Glückes Schmied.

E   Answer the questions by choosing the correct answer.

1. Who generally works outside?

   a. Landwirt   b. Koch

2. Who normally works in an office?

   a. Geschäftsfrau   b. Briefträgerin

3. Who takes care of patients?

   a. Landwirtin   b. Krankenpflegerin

4. Who gives lessons to a group of people?

   a. Lehrer   b. Künstler

5. Who performs in front of people?

   a. Klempner   b. Schauspieler

6. Who cuts wooden beams to size?

   a. Tischler   b. Elektriker

F *Was weißt du?* Similar to our newspapers, you'll find German companies advertising for people who have specific occupations. Read each description and then write the letter of the ad that best fits the description. The following are words that may help you better understand the ads: *suchen* (to look for, want); *gesucht* (wanted); *Maler* (painter[s]); *Verkäuferin* (saleswoman); *Tage pro Woche* (days a week); *freundliche Arzthelferin* (friendly doctor's assistant); *Fleischerei* (butcher shop); *gelernte Fachverkäuferin* (experienced saleswoman); *Flughafen* (airport); *Zahntechniker/in* (dental technician); *versierte Buchhalterin* (experienced bookkeeper).

a
Maler/Elektriker
für Renovierungs-/
Modernisierungsarbeiten sucht
Hueber Personal Leasing
792 90 50 oder 412 50 25

b
Versierte
Buchhalterin
zum baldmöglichsten Eintritt gesucht,
Teilzeitbeschäftigung möglich.
**Fa. GFG Gesellschaft für Grundbe-
sitz mbH, Königswarter Str. 54a,
8510 Fürth, Tel. (09 11) 74 95 25**

c
**Telefon-Marketing
im EDV-Bereich**
Wir suchen per sofort oder später
eine/n **Mitarbeiter/in**
für die Telefonakquisition und Kundenbe-
treuung in uns. Hause in Nürnberg.
Es erwarten Sie eine angenehme Arbeits-
atmosphäre und gute Konditionen.
Sie erreichen uns tel. unter
(09 11) 71 77 59 o. 8 92 06/0

d
Fleischerei Reif in Schöneberg, Hauptstr.
106, Nähe U-Bahnhof Innsbrucker Platz,
sucht gelernte Fachverkäuferin für 2-3
Tage in der Woche, 781 12 15

e
Freundliche Arzthelferin
m. Teamgeist bei guter Bezahlung f. orthopäd. Gemeinschaftspraxis gesucht.
Dr. Wolff/Dr. Valdman,
6230 Ffm.-Höchst, Hostatostr. 13, ☎ 069 / 30 20 85

f
MALERGESELLEN
und *Fachhelfer*
TISCHLER
und *Fachhelfer*
KLEMPNER
mit Berufserfahrung
in Dauerstellung gesucht.
**Stüdemann GmbH
Tel. 882 69 90**

g
Zuverlässiger
Bäcker
ab sofort gesucht.
**Bäckerei Graff, Westerbachstr. 24,
60489 Ffm-Rödelheim T. 069/783647**

h
Wir suchen qualifizierten
Mechaniker
für halbe Tage.
F. + H. Bellinger, Feinmechanik
☎ 061 09 / 3 45 27

i
Zahntechniker/in
f. Edelmetall u. Keramik
gesucht (auch Teilzeit)
— beste Konditionen —
LABOR 1 GmbH-Zahntechnik
☎ 069/553287 u. 591093

j
Wir
ein junges Team mit 8 Mitarbeitern
mit guter Auftragslage und inter-
essanten Projekten im Wohn- und
Gewerbebau
suchen
Architekt/in
mit Schwerpunkt Entwurf,
künstlerischen Fähigkeiten,
Spaß an Teamarbeit,
kreativ und engagiert.
Interessiert? Dann rufen Sie bitte
an, oder senden Sie uns Ihre
Bewerbungsunterlagen.
**Architekturbüro BDA
Hans-Peter Gresser
Nerobergstraße 15
65193 Wiesbaden
Telefon (06 11) 52 00 05**

k
Für unser Restaurant am Flughafen suchen wir einen
KOCH
sowie eine/n
KOCHHELFER/IN
in Dauerstellung. Gute Bezahlung. Schichtdienst.
☎ 0 69 / 690 27 00
werktags zw. 8.00 u. 16.00 Uhr

l
Wir suchen noch eine tüchtige und
zuverlässige
Verkäuferin
3 Tage pro Woche
(für unseren Brotshop im Karstadt,
An der Lorenzkirche)
Bewerben Sie sich bitte telefonisch
unter 09 11 / 3 03 08 16, Montag bis
Freitag 8.00 Uhr bis 15.00 Uhr.

**Großbäckerei WENDELN
GmbH & Co. KG**
Gießener Straße 30
8500 Nürnberg 90

This business/company is...

1. in the renovation business and is looking for painters and electricians. _____

2. looking for qualified mechanics. _____

3. located in Wiesbaden and wants to hire an architect. _____

4. interested in employing a saleswoman three days a week. _____

5. ready to hire a doctor's assistant in Frankfurt-Höchst. _____

6. advertising for a dependable baker. _____

7. a butcher shop looking for a salesperson. _____

8. interested in hiring someone for telemarketing in the Nürnberg area. _____

9. hiring a cook and an assistant cook at an airport restaurant. _____

10. looking for three people, including an experienced plumber. _____

11. looking for a dental technician. _____

12. located in Fürth and is looking for an experienced bookkeeper. _____

G Kreuzworträtsel

Vertical

1. businessman
2. "Was ist...Beruf?"
3. plans menus (f.)
4. repairs automobiles (f.)
5. what the letter carrier carries
6. What do you do?
7. manages a farm
9. draws and paints

Horizontal

3. fixes pipes (m.)
7. instructs pupils
8. diagnoses an illness (f.)
10. interprets musical masterpieces (f.)
11. prepares meals
12. prescribes medicine
13. does carpentry work
14. acts on stage (f.)

H

With a partner play "What's My Line?" in German. Pick one of the occupations whose German name you have learned. Then think of as many German words as you can that have something to do with this occupation. Say these words as clues for your partner, who tries to guess your occupation.

Beispiel You say: Kreide, Schreibtisch, Klassenzimmer

Your partner asks: Bist du Lehrer(in)?

You say: Ja, ich bin Lehrer(in).

Then reverse roles. This time your partner gives you clues and you guess his or her occupation.

Unit 9

A You are thirsty. Circle the items that will quench your thirst.

Kekse	Milch	Messer
Mineralwasser	Abendessen	Käse
Fruchtsaft	Kaffee	Nachtisch
Schokoladenpulver	Bohnen	Tee

B You are hungry. Circle the items that will satisfy your appetite.

Brot	Kuchen	Dose
Tisch	Salz	Verkauf
Apfelsine	Kartoffeln	Kalbsbraten
Birne	Serviette	Liter

C You're having guests for a special dinner this evening. Write all the words *auf deutsch*.

1. Create a nice menu.

   Appetizer: _____ and crackers

   Main Dish (specialty): _____

   Vegetables: _____ and _____

   Dessert: _____

   Beverage(s): _____

2. How many guests will you be serving? _____

3. At what time do you expect to serve the dinner? _____

4. What did you put on the table before you set it? _____

5. What will you say to wish your guests an enjoyable dinner?

   _____

D To keep in good physical shape, one should have a balanced diet. This means (*auf deutsch, bitte*):

1. fruits such as _____ and

   _____ .

2. vegetables such as carrots and _____ .

3. some carbohydrates such as pasta and _____ .

4. some lean meat such as _____ .

5. a calcium-rich beverage such as _____ .

E Wähle die richtige Antwort.

1. Which city is known for honey and spice cake?

   a. Berlin   b. Nürnberg

2. Which city is known for veal cutlets?

   a. Luzern   b. Wien

3. What is the specialty of Königsberg?

   a. fruit dessert   b. meatballs

4. Which region lends its name to a cake?

   a. Schwarzwald   b. Harz

5. In which country is a dish with melted cheese and boiled potatoes a specialty?

   a. die Schweiz   b. Österreich

6. In which city would you most likely eat noodles made of a flour and egg mixture?

   a. Hamburg   b. München

F *Schreib die Wörter richtig.* Unscramble the words.

1. NESES _____

2. SUTRD _____

3. GERHNU _____

4. STOB _____

5. LEPAF _____

6. SEKÄ _____

7. TNÄKEGRE _____

8. ESATS _____

9. ALGBE _____

10. FLÖLFE _____

 G With your partner draw pictures of the foods, beverages and tableware whose German names you have learned. Instead of drawing you may choose to find pictures of these items in back issues of magazines or newspapers. Then cut out these pictures. Take turns with your partner showing a picture as your partner identifies it. Alternate showing and naming objects until all pictures are identified. See who can name the most items correctly.

Beispiel   Your partner shows you a picture of a pineapple.

You say: Ananas

Was weißt du? Let's assume that you work in the city tourist office in Flensburg, located in northern Germany near the Danish border. German and foreign tourists come to your office every day and inquire about restaurants in Flensburg and surrounding areas. As many tourists don't speak German, you describe the various restaurants in English. Tell which restaurants you are describing. Here are some words and expressions that will help you identify each eating establishment: *im Herzen* (in the heart); *Fußgängerzone* (pedestrian zone); *außer* (except); *Bundesstraße* (Federal Highway); *ein weit über Deutschlands Grenzen hinaus bekanntes Restaurant* (a well-known restaurant far beyond Germany's borders); *das preiswerte Selbstauswahl-Restaurant* (the reasonable self-service restaurant); *Sonntags Familien-Brunch* (Sundays family brunch); *bekannt für frischen Fisch* (known for fresh fish); *Mittagstisch* (lunch); *Saal* (large room); *umgeben von Wald und Wasser* (surrounded by forest and water); *Außenterrasse* (outdoor terrace, garden); *griechische Spezialitäten* (Greek specialties); *werktags* (weekdays).

Franchi's Bistro und Café
Große Straße 29, Telefon 2 72 77
Öffnungszeiten: Montag bis Samstag 9.00–22.00 Uhr,
                         Sonntag 13.30–18.00 Uhr
Speisen, Snacks und Eis sowie eine tolle Atmosphäre!
Das Bistro im Herzen der City!
Bei schönem Wetter Straßencafé!

Grundhof-Krug
»Wo Feste feiern Freude macht!«
2391 Grundhof, Telefon (0 46 36) 10 88
Gepflegtes Restaurant in ländlicher Umgebung
Zu empfehlen:
Wild-Spezialitäten, Fischgerichte,
regionale Gerichte wie z. B. »Angeliter Schnüsch«.
Saal für bis zu 200 Personen – Gästezimmer –
Wintergarten – Terrasse
Mittwochs Ruhetag

Restaurant Harmonie
Bekannt für frischen Fisch aus Nord- und Ostsee
Wilhelmstraße 2, Telefon 2 38 41
Täglich geöffnet von 11.00–24.00 Uhr, außer Montag

Historischer Krug
An der Bundesstraße 76
2391 Oeversee,
Telefon (0 46 30) 3 00, Telefax (0 46 30) 7 80
Landessieger »Gastliches Haus« in Schleswig-Holstein,
8 x »Schönes Gasthaus im Kreis«
Hotel und Restaurant mit Komfort

Goloka
Heiligengeistgang 11,
Ecke Große Straße / Fußgängerzone, Telefon 1 38 78
Indisch-vegetarische Spezialitäten, Vollwertkost
Täglich wechselndes Mittagsmenü!
Frische Salate, selbstgemachte indische Süßigkeiten,
Naturkost
Geöffnet von 11.30–18.00 Uhr – außer Samstag
und Sonntag

Taverna Rhodos
Norderstraße 22, Telefon 2 81 06
Griechische Spezialitäten
Öffnungszeiten:
12.00–0.30 Uhr

Schwarzer Walfisch
Angelburger Straße 44, Telefon 2 50 82
Spezialitäten-Restaurant:
Frischfisch der Region, Steaks von A–Z
Ein Besuch ist immer ein Erlebnis!
Geöffnet: Werktags ab 17.00 Uhr

Holmkeller-Restaurants
In der Holmpassage, Holm 39, Telefon 2 40 60
Schlemmer-Karree –
das preiswerte Selbstauswahl-Restaurant mit regionalen
Spezialitäten und Vollwertkost! Bommerlunder Keller –
gepflegte Gastlichkeit in historischen Räumen!
Sonntags Familien-Brunch – Essen Sie, soviel Sie wollen!
Geöffnet von 9.00–22.00 Uhr, sonntags von 10.00–15.00 Uhr

Restaurant und Café »Seeblick«
Am Sankelmarker See, B 76, 2391 Sankelmark
Telefon (0 46 30) 3 77
Dieses direkt an der B 76 gelegene Haus, 8 km von
Flensburg entfernt, umgeben von Wald und Wasser,
bietet Ihnen täglich eine reichhaltige Speisekarte und zum
Kaffee den hausgemachten Kuchen.
Sonnige Außenterrasse

Piet Henningsen
seit 1886
Flensburger Traditionslokal
Besuchen Sie diese älteste Seemannsgaststätte Flensburgs!
Schiffbrücke 20, Telefon 2 45 76
In einmaliger Atmosphäre – mit vielen Souvenirs aus aller
Welt – finden Sie ein weit über Deutschlands Grenzen
hinaus bekanntes Restaurant!
Geöffnet: Montag bis Freitag von 17.00–24.00 Uhr,
Sonnabend und Sonntag von 11.00–24.00 Uhr

Mc Donald's
Große Straße 1, Telefon (04 61) 2 43 44
»Das etwas andere Restaurant«
Sonntag–Donnerstag bis 24.00 Uhr,
Freitag–Samstag bis 1.00 Uhr geöffnet

China-Restaurant »Shanghai«
Friesische Straße 7, Telefon 2 07 86
Wir haben Mittagstisch von DM 5,50 bis DM 10,–
Geöffnet von 12.00–15.00 Uhr und
                         von 18.00–24.00 Uhr

1. This café is open Monday through Saturday from 9 A.M. to 10 P.M. It's located in the heart of the city. _____

2. You'll find this Indian and vegetarian restaurant in the pedestrian zone in the city. It's open every day from 11:30 A.M. until 6 P.M., except on Saturdays and Sundays.

   _____

3. It's a historical restaurant located right on Federal Highway 76. You will find the restaurant in the hotel itself. _____

4. This traditional restaurant is one of the oldest establishments in Flensburg as it was founded in 1886. It's known far beyond Germany's borders as a fine restaurant.

   _____

5. If you and your family enjoy Sunday brunches, then this self-service restaurant with its reasonable prices is the place to go. It's open on Sundays from 10 A.M. to 3 P.M. and you can eat as much as you want. _____

6. If you like fresh fish from the North and Baltic Seas, you may want to go to this place. It's open every day, except on Mondays. _____

7. This eating establishment is known all over the world. If you want to eat there, you'll find it in the *Große Straße*. It's open every day.

   _____

8. Should you like Chinese food, I would recommend eating there at noon. Their lunch prices are quite reasonable. They range from 5.50 marks to 10 marks.

   _____

9. If you have a big tour group with you, this restaurant can offer you a large room for up to 200 people. However, you should make reservations well in advance by calling this number: 04636 1088. _____

10. Just like the other restaurant I mentioned, this one is also located on the Federal Highway 76. It's surrounded by a forest and water and offers an outdoor terrace.

    _____

11. In case you enjoy Greek food, you may wish to consider this restaurant located in the *Norderstraße*. However, it doesn't open until noon.

    _____

12. This restaurant specializes in steaks. Unfortunately, it's not open on weekends. You may want to call for reservations. The phone number is 25082.

    _____

Unit 10

A For each item, put a check in the column of the appropriate artist(s).

	Albrecht Dürer	Caspar David Friedrich	Ernst Ludwig Kirchner	Franz Marc
1. *The Young Hare*				
2. *Ships in the Harbor of Greifswald*				
3. *Street, Berlin*				
4. "Brücke"				
5. romanticism				
6. expressionism				
7. classicism				
8. cityscapes				
9. seascapes				
10. religion and war				
11. vivid colors				
12. Nürnberg				
13. Dresden				
14. München				
15. Greifswald				

B Name the artists.

1. If you like unusual colors and shapes, you might like the artworks of

_____ and

_____ .

2. If you like fine detail in a picture, you might enjoy the artworks of

_____ .

3. If you like pictures which affect you emotionally, you might prefer the artworks of

_____ .

Name: _____ Datum: _____

C Was paßt zusammen?

1. Artist, who studied in Dresden, was born. _____   a. 1913
2. Wood carver from Nürnberg died that year. _____   b. 1911
3. *Lone Tree* was created that year. _____   c. 1840
4. *The Young Hare* dates back to that year. _____   d. 1528
5. This North German painter died that year. _____   e. 1502
6. The oil painting *Street, Berlin* was completed. _____   f. 1880
7. This Renaissance artist was born that year. _____   g. 1471
8. *The Large Blue Horses* goes back to that year. _____   h. 1823

D Draw each item named.

1. ein Buch   2. ein Haus

3. eine Ananas   4. ein Apfel

5. eine Gabel   6. ein Teller

E Draw a picture to show what each person is doing.

1. Stefan ißt (*is eating*) eine Apfelsine.

2. Antje hebt die Hand.

3. Maria schreibt mit einem Kuli.

4. Daniel spricht mit dem Briefträger.

F   Kreuzworträtsel

Vertical

2. painting by Dürer, 1502
3. Dürer's painting style
5. city associated with C. D. Friedrich
7. This unit is about three German...
8. *The Four Horsemen* is a woodcut by...
10. *The...Blue Horses*
11. Franz...
13. The opposite of country life is...life.
15. C. D. Friedrich painted many landscapes and...scapes.

Horizontal

1. This saint is the subject of Dürer's copper engraving.
4. oil painting of 1823 by C. D. Friedrich
6. The ships are in the...Greifswald.
8. E. L. Kirchner studied art in this city.
9. city associated with A. Dürer
12. romantic painter
14. color of the horses painted by Marc
16. pedestians on a busy...in Berlin

G Of the six pictures you have studied in this unit, *The Young Hare*; *Saint Anthony*; *The Large Blue Horses*; *Street, Berlin*; *Ships in the Harbor of Greifswald* and *Lone Tree*, decide which one is your favorite. Your teacher will designate an area of your classroom as one of these six paintings. Go to the area that represents your favorite picture. Pair up with a partner. Each of you tells the other why you like this painting the best. Then get together with another pair of students in your area so that you can tell the new pair why your partner prefers this painting. Finally, a spokesperson from each of the six groups tells the entire class why students from that group prefer that picture.

H *Was weißt du?* Match the name of each museum with its appropriate description. All museums are in Augsburg, located in southern Germany. Some useful words to know are: *Eintritt frei, freier Eintritt* (no entrance fee); *Montags geschlossen* (closed on Mondays); *Geschichte der Entwicklung des Dieselmotors* (history of the development of the diesel motor); *bis auf weiteres geschlossen* (closed until further notice); *Stadt- und Handwerksgeschichte* (history of city and handicrafts); *geöffnet letzter Samstag im Monat* (open on the last Saturday of the month).

Maximilianmuseum und Diözesan-museum, Philippine-Welser-Straße 24
Plastik, Kunstgewerbe, Stadt- und Handwerksgeschichte

MAN-Werkmuseum, Heinrich-von-Buz-Straße 28, Telefon 3 22-37 91
Dokumentation der Entwicklung des Werkes Augsburg und der Augsburger Produktionsbereiche. Geschichte der Entwicklung des Dieselmotors.
Öffnungszeiten: Mo bis Fr von 8–16 Uhr.

Römisches Museum, Dominikanergasse 15 (in der ehem. Dominikanerkirche)
Sammlung vorgeschichtlicher, römerzeitlicher und frühgeschichtlicher Funde aus Augsburg und Bayerisch Schwaben – Antike Kleinkunst aus dem Mittelmeergebiet.

Museen der Städtischen Kunstsammlungen Augsburg
Mai bis September 10–17 Uhr, Oktober bis April 10–16 Uhr geöffnet. Montags geschlossen. Eintritt 3,– DM, Ermäßigungen. Jeden 1. Sonntag im Monat freier Eintritt.

Heimatmuseum Stadt und Landkreis Neudek, Von-Cobres-Straße 5,
Telefon 9 25 31/92386
Geöffnet letzter Samstag im Monat 14–17 Uhr und nach Vereinbarung.

Schwäbisches Volkskundemuseum Oberschönenfeld, Telefon 0 82 38-45 45
Öffnungszeiten: Mi, Sa, So 10–17 Uhr.

Naturmuseum, Im Thäle 3,
bis auf weiteres geschlossen.

Synagoge und Jüdisches Kultur-museum, Halderstr. 6–8, Tel. 51 79 85
10. Mai bis 22. Juni. Marc Chagall: „Die Bibel" – Radierungen. Geöffnet: Di, Do, Fr 10–15 Uhr, Mi 15–20 Uhr, So 10–17 Uhr.

Schwäbisches Handwerksmuseum
im Brunnenmeisterhaus beim Roten Tor,
Telefon 32 59-2 24
Mo bis Fr jeweils 14–18 Uhr und sonntags von 10–18 Uhr geöffnet, Eintritt frei.

1.   Maximilianmuseum und Diözesanmuseum   _____

2.   MAN-Werkmuseum   _____

3.   Römisches Museum   _____

4.   Museen der Städtischen Kunstsammlungen Augsburg   _____

5.   Heimatmuseum Stadt und Landkreis Neudek   _____

6.   Schwäbisches Volkskundemuseum Oberschönenfeld _____

7.   Synagoge und Jüdisches Kulturmuseum   _____

8.   Naturmuseum   _____

9.   Schwäbisches Handwerksmuseum   _____

This museum...

   a.   is open three days a week from 10 A.M. until 5 P.M.
   b.   is located in the *Dominikanergasse*.
   c.   is open for eight hours on Sundays and there is no entrance fee.
   d.   is open Mondays through Fridays from 8 A.M. to 4 P.M. The museum documents the history of the development of the diesel motor.
   e.   is closed until further notice.
   f.   is closed on Mondays. Entrance fee is 3 marks, except every first Sunday of the month, when entrance is free of charge.
   g.   has a Marc Chagall exhibit from May 10 through June 22.
   h.   exhibits items relating to the history of the city and handicrafts.
   i.   is open only on the last Saturday of the month.

Name: _____ Datum: _____

Unit 11

 A Do you know your *Körperteile*? Match column B with column A.

A		B
1. hair _____		a. der Fuß
2. nose _____		b. das Ohr
3. foot _____		c. das Knie
4. chest _____		d. der Kopf
5. neck _____		e. die Nase
6. elbow _____		f. die Brust
7. ear _____		g. der Hals
8. eye _____		h. der Ellenbogen
9. knee _____		i. das Haar
10. head _____		j. das Auge

B Answer the questions *auf deutsch.*

Which part of your body...

1. lets you know that something is baking in the oven? _____

2. is brushed to avoid cavities? _____

3. bends to help you sit? _____

4. lets you play the piano? _____

5. stores your brain? _____

C Odd one out! Circle the item that doesn't fit the description on the left.

1. Geh an die Tafel. Fuß Ellenbogen

2. Schreib. Kinn Hand

3. Lies. Stirn Auge

4. Hör zu. Brust Ohr

5. Sprich. Zehe Mund

D Ergänze die fehlenden Buchstaben!

1. die ____chulter

2. der A____m

3. der Hal____

4. das Kni____

5. der ____und

6. das Gesic____t

7. die S____irn

8. der Ba____ch

9. das ____ein

10. das Ha____r

E All these people have aches and pains! Do you know what's wrong with them? Look for the *Körperteil* that hurts and figure out the problem.

1. Ali hat Bauchschmerzen. _____

2. Reyhan hat Zahnschmerzen. _____

3. Das Ohr tut Heiko weh. _____

4. Der Kopf tut Lore weh. _____

5. Der Hals tut Michael weh. _____

F   Kreuzworträtsel

Vertical

2. what you lend or give
3. what you see in the mirror
4. lets you hear things
6. above your eyebrows
9. what you put into your shoe (SS=ß)
10. parts of the body
13. lets you smell things
14. leg joint

Horizontal

1. what hurts if you eat too much
5. lets you see things
7. used for walking and swimming
8. top part of your arm
10. lower end of your face
11. between your neck and abdomen
12. upper and lower part of the mouth
15. lets you lift and throw
16. top part of your head
17. front part of your foot
18. midpoint between hand and shoulder
19. what holds your head up

Name: _____ Datum: _____

G Challenge your partner by asking him or her to identify parts of the body and to spell each one. For example, point to your nose and ask your partner the question "*Was ist das?*" If your partner says "*Das ist die Nase,*" he or she gets one point. Then ask your partner "*Wie buchstabiert man das Wort?*" (How do you spell the word?) If your partner spells the word correctly, for example, "*N...A...S...E...,*" (in German, if possible), he or she gets another point. Then, your partner will ask you the name of a body part ("*Was ist das?*"), and if you know, he or she will also ask you to spell it ("*Wie buchstabiert man das Wort?*"). Both of you should attempt to identify and spell at least five body parts. Whoever has the most points is the winner.

H *Was weißt du?* Imagine that you have been invited to participate on the German TV show called *Jeopardy*. It's now your turn. There are several categories to choose from. The quizmaster asks you to select one. After looking over the various categories, you decide to select the category called *Körperteile*. As the other competing participants speak English, the quizmaster reads all the sentences in English, but asks you to identify each part of the body in German. If you identify all the words correctly including the articles (*der, die* or *das*), you'll be the grand-prize winner. Can you do it?

Körperteile		
1. The part of the face that bears the nostrils and covers the anterior part of the nasal cavity. _____	5. The part of the upper body that contains the brain and the mouth. _____	9. The part of the body that is also sometimes called the "abdomen" or "belly." _____
2. The last part of the leg upon which a person stands. _____	6. The joint in the middle part of the leg. _____	10. The part that is located below the lower lip and above the neck. _____
3. The organ that makes it possible to hear. _____	7. The organ that makes it possible to see. _____	11. The part between the shoulder and the wrist. _____
4. One of the five terminating members of the hand. _____	8. The opening through which food is passed. _____	12. The part that connects the head with the body. _____

Unit 12

A Write in German what you...

1. wear over your pyjamas. _____

2. wear on your hands. _____

3. need to blow your nose. _____

4. need to secure your skirt or pants. _____

5. wear on your head. _____

B Finish each sentence with the name of an article of clothing. The first letter of each word is started for you.

1. Astrid hat ein K_____ an.

2. Ich habe einem warmen M_____ an.

3. Mohammed hat ein H_____ und eine

   H_____ an.

4. Jutta hat eine J_____ an.

C What's the price? Finish each sentence with the German word for each item in parentheses.

1. Wieviel kostet die _____? (blouse)

2. Wieviel kostet der _____? (suit)

3. Wieviel kostet die _____? (cardigan sweater)

4. Wieviel kosten die _____? (shoes)

5. Wieviel kosten die _____? (hats)

D Odd one out! Which item doesn't fit? Circle.

1. Handschuhe	Hut	Krawatte
2. Schuhe	Bluse	Pantoffeln
3. Hut	Rock	Hose
4. Moden	Gürtel	Taschentuch
5. Hemd	Jacke	Socken

E Match column B with column A.

A		B
1. dressy attire for girl _____		a. Bluse
2. formal attire for boy _____		b. Krawatte
3. bedtime outfit _____		c. Schlafanzug
4. decorative item for boy _____		d. Kleid
5. fancy shirt for girl _____		e. Anzug

F Who wears what and where? Begin by thinking of five names of occupations in German. Say each occupation and your partner will say what someone who has that job typically wears.

Beispiel   You say: Lehrerin

Your partner says: Bluse, Rock, Schuhe

Then it's your partner's turn. He or she thinks of five names of places in German. After he or she says each one, you will say what someone in that location typically wears.

Beispiel   Your partner says: Schlafzimmer

You say: Bademantel, Pantoffeln

G *Was weißt du?* Complete the sentences that follow by reading the five ads.

1. The price for the *Hüttenschuhe für Kinder* is _____

   marks a pair.

2. The specialty shop that is selling the *Brand Moden* is located in the city of

   _____ .

3. If you want to call the store *Pelz & Leder* which specializes in fur coats, you can dial

   _____ .

4. Ladies' or men's pullovers are advertized at DM 39,98 each for sizes S through

   _____ .

5. The *Herren Inka-Jacke*, advertized at 99 marks, is available in

   _____ different color combinations

   (*verschiedenen Farbkombinationen*).

6. The *Pelz & Leder* store opens on Saturdays (*Sa. = Samstag*) at

   _____ A.M.

7. A three-quarter length man's leather jacket (*Herren-Lederjacke*) can be purchased in

   sizes _____ to 58.

8. The *Brand Moden* shop has a department that sells wedding dresses, tuxedos and

   evening gowns in an area that has a sales floor of more than

   _____ m² (square meters).

9. The children's pajamas (*Kinder-Schlafanzug*) have _____

   percent cotton (*Baumwolle*).

10. *Pelz & Leder* is located in _____ -Niedersteinbach.

H Find your way through the clothing store. Name each item of clothing (*auf deutsch, bitte*) you encounter as you leave the store.

_____   _____

_____   _____

_____   _____

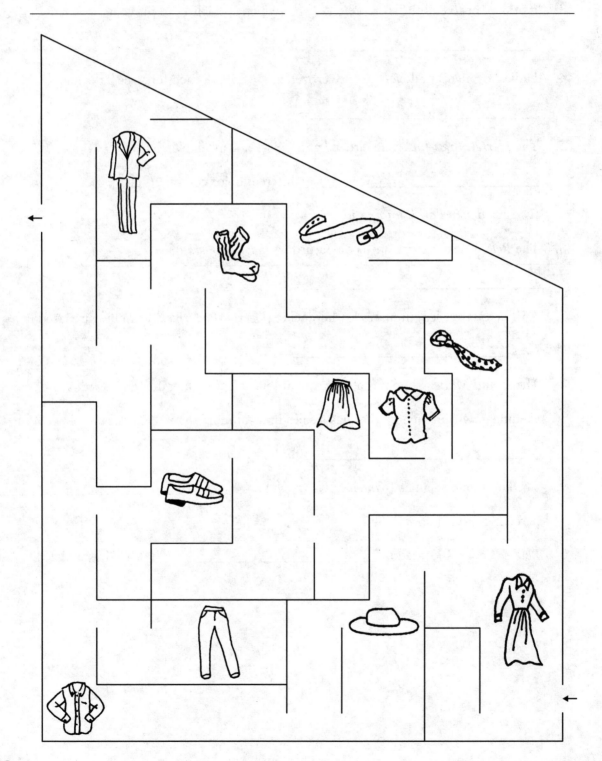

Unit 13

A *Welche Farbe?* Identify the color of each item. (*Auf deutsch, bitte.*)

1. raspberries _____

2. rain clouds _____

3. snowballs _____

4. sunflowers _____

5. crows _____

6. "Käse" _____

7. "Milch" _____

8. "Spinat" _____

9. "Apfelsine" _____

10. "Kaffee" _____

B Answer each question by circling the appropriate time. Watch out for <u>official</u> times!

1. At what time does the sun set?

   a. um zwei Uhr   b. um neunzehn Uhr

2. At what time do you leave for school in the morning?

   a. um dreizehn Uhr   b. um halb acht

3. At what time does the afternoon movie start?

   a. um vierzehn Uhr   b. um zehn Uhr

4. At what time does the sun rise?

   a. um sechs Uhr zwei   b. um zwei Uhr sechs

5. What time is good for star-gazing?

   a. ein Uhr   b. einundzwanzig Uhr

C Rewrite the colors in the wordbox according to the shade, from darkest at the left to lightest at the right.

violett	weiß	gelb	rot	grün

darkest   lightest

D What time is it? Write the numeral form of each statement.

1. Es ist Viertel vor zwölf.   _____

2. Es ist halb vier.   _____

3. Es ist zwanzig Uhr.   _____

4. Es ist ein Uhr.   _____

5. Es ist siebzehn Minuten nach fünf.   _____

E Color combinations. Each color on the left is a combination of two other colors. Do you know what these are? *Auf deutsch, bitte!*

1. grün   = _____ + _____

2. orange = _____ + _____

3. grau   = _____ + _____

4. rosa   = _____ + _____

5. violett = _____ + _____

F Kreuzwortr ä tsel

Vertical

1. time when sun is at highest point in the sky
2. color of tomatoes and cranberries
3. color of India ink and pepper
4. colors
5. 60 make an hour
6. color of clouds when it's nice out (SS=ß)
8. boy's dress-up outfit
10. 20 - 1 =...
15. "Wieviel...ist es?"
18. "Es...neun Uhr."

Horizontal

2. mixture of red and white
5. time between P.M. and A.M.
7. color of forget-me-nots
9. color of string and lima beans
11. "eins, zwei,..."
12. "Wieviel Uhr ist...?"
13. color of carrots and pumpkins
14. color of smoke and ashes
16. color of corn and dandelions
17. "Sechs Weniger zwei =..."
19. "Du hast...Finger."
20. time

G With your partner take turns making quick sketches like the one in the example that show the time. Add a moon or a sun to your drawing to indicate the difference between A.M. and P.M. Ask your partner the time and he or she will answer you based on your sketch.

Beispiel

You show this sketch to your partner and ask: Wieviel Uhr ist es?

Your partner answers: Es ist neun Uhr.

H *Was weißt du?* It's quite common in Germany to travel by train. At train stations you'll find detailed train schedules between major cities. These schedules contain many items such as indicated in the train schedule between the cities of Wiesbaden and Hannover. This schedule contains only the trains that operate in the morning until around noon. The back (not shown here) continues with departure/arrival details for the remaining part of the day.

Here are the explanations of some of the important abbreviations and words you need to know to answer the questions that follow: *km* (kilometer[s]), *Umsteigen* (transfer), *Verkehrszeiten* (transportation time), *ab* (departure at), *Zug* (train), *an* (arrival at), *So- u Feiertage* (Sundays and Holidays), *Mo bis Sa* (Monday through Saturday), *Mo bis Fri* (Monday through Friday), *werktags außer...* (weekdays except...), *täglich* (daily), *Ffm* (abbreviation for "Frankfurt").

Fahrplanauszug   **DB**

Wiesbaden → Hannover   398 km

Verkehrszeiten	ab	Zug	an	Service	Umsteigen in	an	ab	Zug
	4.42	Ⓢ	9.31		Ffm	5.33	6.26	E3802
					Fulda	7.48	8.06	ICE684
So- u Feiertage, auch 10.VI.	5.07	Ⓢ	9.31		Ffm	5.46	6.26	E3802
					Fulda	7.48	8.06	ICE684
Mo bis Sa, nicht 31.V., 10.VI., 25.XII. bis 2.I., 2. bis 4.IV., 23.V.	5.27	Ⓢ •	8.38		Ffm	6.06	6.17	ICE798
Mo bis Fr, nicht 31.V., 24.XII. bis 2.I., 1. bis 4.IV., 23.V.	5.30	ICE674	8.14	Bes. Tarif ✗				
Mo bis Sa, nicht 31.V., 25.XII. bis 2.I., 2. bis 4.IV., 23.V.	6.16	IC608	11.03	✗				
	6.42	Ⓢ	10.06		Ffm	7.33	7.51	ICE672
werktags außer Sa, nicht 10.VI., 24., 31.XII.	7.01	E3151	10.06		Ffm	7.34	7.51	ICE672
	7.39	IC911	10.38		Ffm	8.07	8.18	ICE796
	8.43	Ⓢ	12.06		Ffm	9.33	9.50	ICE690
	9.39	IC913	12.38		Ffm	10.07	10.18	ICE794
	9.59	IC955	14.06		Mainz	10.09	10.38	IC725
					Ffm	11.08	11.51	ICE772
werktags, nicht 10.VI.	10.36	E3153	14.06		Ffm	11.07	11.51	ICE772
So- u Feiertage, auch 10.VI.	10.42	Ⓢ	14.06		Ffm	11.33	11.51	ICE772
	11.39	IC915	14.38		Ffm	12.07	12.18	ICE898
	11.59	IC959	16.00		Mainz	12.09	12.38	IC727
					Ffm	13.08	13.18	ICE596
					KS-Wilhelm	14.42	15.00	IC780
täglich außer Sa, nicht 30.V., 24.XII. bis 1.I., 1. bis 3.IV., 22.V.	11.59	IC959	16.06		Mainz	12.09	12.38	IC727
					Ffm	13.08	13.51	ICE576
werktags, nicht 10.VI.	12.27	Ⓢ	16.00		Ffm	13.06	13.18	ICE596
					KS-Wilhelm	14.42	15.00	IC780
So- u Feiertage, nicht 30.V., 24.XII. bis 1.I., 1. bis 3.IV., 22.V.	12.36	Ⓢ	16.06		Ffm	13.33	13.51	ICE576

1. What is the distance between Wiesbaden and Hannover?

   _____

2. At what time does the Intercity (IC) train that leaves Wiesbaden at 6:16 A.M. arrive in Hannover?

   _____

3. At what time does train ICE772 leave Frankfurt?

   _____

4. In which city do you have to transfer when you leave Wiesbaden via train IC915?

   _____

5. How many hours and minutes does it take to go from Wiesbaden to Hannover via Mainz on train IC959, and continue on train IC727 to Hannover?

   _____

6. Which train leaves Fulda at 8:06 A.M.?

   _____

7. At what time does the earliest train leave from Frankfurt for Hannover?

   _____

8. How many minutes does it take by train from Wiesbaden to Mainz?

   _____

9. Do you have to transfer on train ICE674 going from Wiesbaden to Hannover?

   _____

10. At what time does the last train (listed in the schedule) depart from Frankfurt on most Sundays and holidays?

    _____

11. Does train E3151 operate every day?

    _____

12. On what days does the train leave Wiesbaden at 10:36 A.M.?

    _____

Name: _____   Datum: _____

Unit 14

A Identify each music work by name.

1. seasonal holiday music

_____

2. opera about a musical instrument

_____

3. concertos from a certain place

_____

4. symphony about nature and beauty

_____

5. symphony in honor of a Roman god

_____

B Name a musician associated with each place.

1. Leipzig   _____

2. Salzburg   _____

3. Bonn   _____

4. Eisenach   _____

5. Vienna   _____

C Guess who...

1. as a child entertained kings and queens.

    _____

2. started his career as a church organist.

    _____

3. spent most of his life as a church organist.

    _____

4. liked freedom and democratic ideals.

    _____

5. taught youngsters how to sing.

    _____

D Unscramble the names.

1. GWUIDL   _____

2. NONJAH   _____

3. GFALOWNG   _____

4. SIBNEASTA   _____

5. UDMAASE   _____

E Kreuzworträtsel

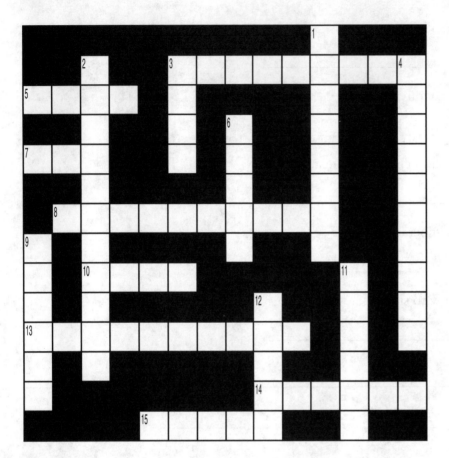

Vertical

1. first name of composer who was born in Salzburg
2. ...*Concertos*
3. musician who was at least 60 years old when he died
4. *Eine Kleine*....
6. *The Magic*....
9. His...educated Mozart.
11. *Eine...Nachtmusik*
12. Mozart was buried in a pauper's....

Horizontal

3. musician who studied in Vienna
5. Bach was...in Eisenach.
7. Ludwig...Beethoven
8. This musician became interested in the democratic ideals of the French....
10. Beethoven was an organist at the Elector's court in....
13. Bach could play several musical instruments such as the violin, the organ and the....
14. Beethoven became a well-known musician in the Austrian city of....
15. "Sie spielt die erste...."

F Interview your partner about his or her musical tastes. Ask your partner the following questions and note his or her answers. Then reverse roles so that your partner interviews you.

1. What is your favorite type of music?

   _____

   _____

2. Who are your favorite male and female singers?

   _____

   _____

3. Who is your favorite group?

   _____

   _____

4. Can you name a singer or group from outside the U.S.?

   _____

   _____

5. Have you ever seen any singers or groups in concert? If so, which singer(s) or group(s)?

   _____

   _____

6. Do you play any musical instruments? If so, which one(s)?

   _____

   _____

G *Was weißt du?* Every German city has numerous opportunities for local people and visitors to be exposed to a variety of stage performances ranging from operas to ballets to plays. See how much you understand in reading the five-day schedule that lists performances to take place in three different areas of Frankfurt. Here are some words that you may want to know when filling in the information for the sentences that follow: *Samstag* (Saturday), *Sonntag* (Sunday), *Montag* (Monday), *Mittwoch* (Wednesday), *Donnerstag* (Thursday), *in Vorbereitung* (in preparation), *keine Vorstellung* (no performance), *...zieht um* (is parading).

Städtische Bühnen Frankfurt am Main **Oper Ballett Schauspiel**
STADT FRANKFURT AM MAIN

	GROSSES HAUS Theaterplatz · Oper · Ballett	**BOCKENHEIMER DEPOT** Bockenheimer Warte · Schauspiel	**KAMMERSPIEL** Hofstraße · Schauspiel
SAMSTAG **1**	**New Sleep /** Ballett Frankfurt 20.00–22.00 Uhr **Die Befragung** freier Verkauf **des Robert Scott †/** **Skinny** Choreographien von William Forsythe Musik von Tom Willems Das Ballettensemble	**Schauspiel Frankfurt** **zieht um! Ziehen Sie mit!** Start um 12.00 Uhr auf dem Theaterplatz Ankunft am Bockenheimer Depot ca. 13.45 Uhr Information, Musik, Aktion	Premiere **Krankheit der** 20.00 Uhr **Jugend** von Ferdinand Bruckner **Die Gerechten** von Albert Camus Leitung: Laufenberg, Jäkel, Géraud mit Esser, Marschall, Schulz / Gerber, Labmeier, Leja, Quast, Schlegelberger
SONNTAG **2**	**Museumskonzert** Alte Oper · 11.00 Uhr **Europeras 1 & 2** 19.30–22.00 Uhr Abo E von John Cage freier Verkauf Andreou, Shamir, Page, Card, Rørholm, Schlemm, Gramatzki, Neubauer, Beckwitt, Williams, Tenge, Kersten / Müller, Ruohonen, Workman, Hagenau, Bachlund, Jar, Glücksmann, Mora, Zinovenko, Vesco, Bavoni, Laube, Senn, Hoffmann, Schmitt, Ernie, Kühl		**Krankheit der** 20.00 Uhr **Jugend** von Ferdinand Bruckner **Die Gerechten** von Albert Camus Leitung und Besetzung wie am 1. Oktober 1988
MONTAG **3**	**Museumskonzert** Alte Oper · 20.00 Uhr **New Sleep /** Ballett Frankfurt 20.00–22.00 Uhr **Die Befragung** freier Verkauf **des Robert Scott †/** **Skinny** Choreographien von William Forsythe Musik von Tom Willems Das Ballettensemble	Bockenheimer Depot U6 U7 19 33 Haltestelle Bockenheimer Warte	Wiederaufnahme **Der** 20.00–21.50 Uhr **Kontrabass** von Patrick Süskind Leitung: Günther, Jäkel mit Hans-Jörg Assmann
MITTWOCH **5**	**Europeras 1 & 2** 19.30–22.00 Uhr Abo B von John Cage freier Verkauf Andreou, Shamir, Page, Card, Rørholm, Schlemm, Gramatzki, Neubauer, Beckwitt, Williams, Tenge, Kersten / Müller, Ruohonen, Mayer, Hagenau, Bachlund, Jar, Workman, Glücksmann, Mora, Zinovenko, Vesco, Bavoni, Laube, Senn, Hoffmann, Schmitt, Ernie, Kühl		Keine Vorstellung
DONNERSTAG **6**	**Der** 19.30–22.45 Uhr **Wildschütz** freier Verkauf von Albert Lortzing Olbrich – Kaufmann, Gramatzki, Freyler, M. Graf / Karczykowski, Workman, Schwanbeck, Krause, Gorstelle	In Vorbereitung **Leben Eduards** **des Zweiten von England** von Marlowe / Brecht / Feuchtwanger	Wiederaufnahme **Vor dem** 20.00–23.00 Uhr **Ruhestand** von Thomas Bernhard Leitung: Heigl, Gelhaar, Lehr mit Engelmann, Strien / Schwuchow

1. The concert *Europeras 1 & 2* in the *Großes Haus* takes place on (name the two days during the week) _____ .

2. Ferdinand Bruckner wrote (title of play)

   _____ .

3. The ballet on Saturday starts at (time) _____ .

4. The play _____

   is currently in preparation.

5. The schedule specifically states that there is no Wednesday performance at the (name of theater) _____ .

6. There is a parade on Saturday that starts at noon at the (name of square)

   _____ .

7. Patrick Süskind's play ends at (time) _____ .

8. The music in the Monday performance in the *Großes Haus* was composed by (name)

   _____ .

9. The play (title) _____

   is under the direction of Heigl, Gelhaar and Lehr with Engelmann, Strien and Schwuchow.

10. The performance on Thursday in the *Großes Haus* starts at (time)

    _____ .

11. Glücksmann is a person who is involved in the performance of (title)

    _____ .

12. The premiere performance (*Premiere*) of Albert Camus' play *Die Gerechten* takes place on (day of week) _____ .

Unit 15

A Name a season when the following weather is typical.

1. Es ist heiß.   _____

2. Es ist windig und es regnet.   _____

3. Es schneit.   _____

4. Es ist windig und kalt.   _____

5. Es ist schwül.   _____

B Explain your reasons in German for advising someone what to pack or do.

1. Take warm clothing because:

    im Winter ist es in Berlin _____ .

2. Take light-weight clothing because:

    im Sommer ist es in München _____ .

3. Take a coat and a hat because:

    im Herbst ist es in Wien _____ und

    _____ .

4. Take an umbrella because:

    im Frühling _____ es oft in Deutschland.

5. When there is an electrical storm, stay inside because:

    _____ .

Name: _____ Datum: _____

C Match Column B with Column A.

A		B	
1. Es schneit. _____		a.	sun
2. Wetter _____		b.	It's raining.
3. Frühling _____		c.	weather
4. kalt _____		d.	It's snowing.
5. schlecht _____		e.	windy
6. Sonne _____		f.	bad
7. windig _____		g.	cold
8. Es regnet. _____		h.	spring

D Name a season when...

1. some birds fly south. _____

2. some animals hibernate. _____

3. the shade feels better than the sun. _____

4. the air gets warmer and the snow starts to melt. _____

5. you carve pumpkins. _____

E Name a weather condition associated with each cue.

1. lawn chair _____

2. toboggan _____

3. lilacs _____

4. snowsuit _____

5. rakes _____

6. perspiration _____

7. electricity _____

8. noise in the sky _____

Name: _____ Datum: _____

F   Find your way through the seasons. Using the pictures as cues, write down the weather conditions you encounter.

_____   _____

_____   _____

_____   _____

_____   _____

_____   _____

                           _____

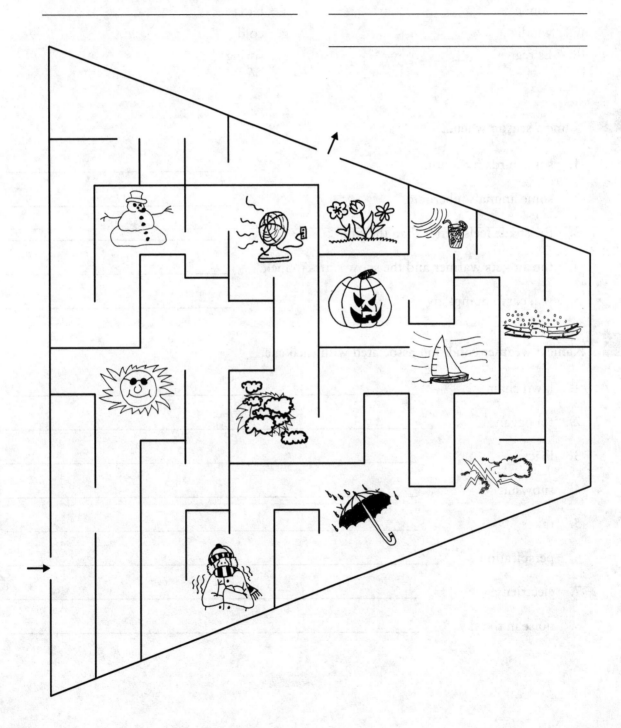

G Make a list of as many German sentences as you can that describe the weather. Say each sentence as a clue for your partner. He or she will say the name of the appropriate season in German and also will list the clothing suitable for that season.

Beispiel   You say: Es schneit.

Your partner says: Es ist Winter. Wollkleid, Strickjacke, Handschuhe, Mantel.

After you have said each of your sentences, reverse roles. Now your partner gives you clues and you tell the season and the appropriate clothing.

H *Was weißt du?* Being able to read a weather report becomes an important function, especially if you are planning outdoor activities. The weather information in this activity provides you with specific details of weather conditions in Europe. Remember that temperatures in Europe are measured in centigrade (*Celsius*). To convert centigrade to Fahrenheit, multiply by 9, divide by 5 and add 32. (Example: $20°C = 20 × 9 ÷ 5 + 32 = 68°F$) Can you give the answers in the statements that follow? Here are a few words you need to know: *Wettervorhersage* (weather forecast), *Regen* (rain), *Sonnenaufgang* (sunrise), *stark bewölkt* (heavily clouded), *wolkenlos* (no clouds), *Monduntergang* (moonset), *Regenschauer* (rain shower[s]).

Das Wetter

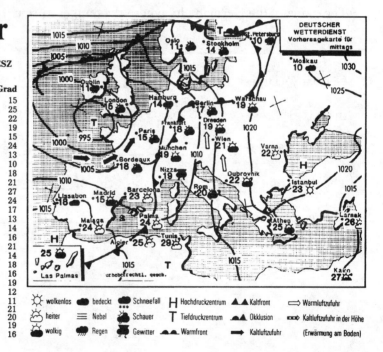

Wetterdaten vom Vortag, 14 Uhr MESZ

Ausland

Ort	Wetter	Grad
Amsterdam	wolkig	15
Athen	wolkig	25
Barcelona	wolkig	22
Bordeaux	stark bewölkt	19
Brüssel	leicht bewölkt	15
Budapest	wolkig	24
Dublin	stark bewölkt	13
Helsinki	leicht bewölkt	10
Innsbruck	wolkig	18
Istanbul	wolkenlos	21
Larnaka	leicht bewölkt	27
Las Palmas	leicht bewölkt	24
Lissabon	leicht bewölkt	17
London	stark bewölkt	13
Madrid	wolkig	14
Malaga	Regenschauer	16
Mallorca	bedeckt	21
Moskau	wolkenlos	14
Nizza	stark bewölkt	18
Paris	wolkig	16
Prag	leicht bewölkt	19
St. Petersburg	leicht bewölkt	12
Stockholm	Regen	11
Venedig	wolkig	21
Warschau	leicht bewölkt	20
Wien	wolkig	19
Zürich	leicht bewölkt	16

Deutschland

Ort	Wetter	Grad
Berlin	wolkig	17
Dresden	wolkig	17
Feldberg/Schw.	leicht bewölkt	8
Feldberg/Ts.	leicht bewölkt	10
Frankfurt/M.	leicht bewölkt	17
Freiburg	leicht bewölkt	20
Garmisch	leicht bewölkt	15
Hamburg	leicht bewölkt	16
Helgoland	wolkig	14
Köln/Bonn	wolkig	15
Leipzig	wolkig	17
München	leicht bewölkt	18
Norderney	stark bewölkt	14
Rostock	wolkig	17
Sylt	leicht bewölkt	14
Zugspitze	in Wolken	−1

Telefonansagedienste

Wettervorhersage	11 64
Reisewettervorhersage	1 16 00
Segelflugwetter	1 15 06
Medizinisch-meteorologische Tips, unter anderem für Allergiker und Herz-Kreislauf-Patienten	1 16 01

Zwei-Tages-Prognose (verbesserte Wettervorhersage zum Preis von fünf Gebühreneinheiten pro Minute):

Deutschland	0190-11 64 00
Regionen: Schleswig-Holstein/Hamburg/Niedersachsen/Bremen	0190-11 64-02,

Mecklenburg-Vorpommern/ Brandenburg/Berlin -03, Nordrhein-Westfalen -04, Hessen/Rheinland-Pfalz/Saarland -05, Thüringen/Sachsen-Anhalt/Sachsen -06, Baden-Württemberg -07 und Bayern

	0190-11 64 08
Reisewetter	0190-11 64 20
Wochenwetterprognose	0190-11 64 50
Ozonwerte	06 11 - 58 12 42

Wenn die Grenzwerte überschritten werden, melden wir dies an gesonderter Stelle.

Sonnenaufgang	6.36 Uhr
Sonnenuntergang	17.49 Uhr
Mondaufgang	22.51 Uhr
Monduntergang	13.48 Uhr

1. The temperature in München is _____ °C.

2. The weather in Madrid is _____ .

3. The phone number for the weather forecast is _____ .

4. The temperature on the island of Helgoland is 14°C which is

    _____ °F.

5. The city where it's raining and the temperature is 11°C is

    _____ .

6. The sun rises at _____ A.M.

7. The French city where it's heavily clouded and the temperature is 18°C is

    _____ .

8. The name of the German city where the temperature is 16°C is

    _____ .

9. Germany's largest mountain is _____ . The temperature

    there is -1°C.

10. The moon sets at _____ P.M.

11. There are rain showers in the Spanish city of _____ .

12. The temperature in Dresden is _____ °C.

Unit 16

A Rearrange the days of the week in the usual sequence. Start with the German word for Monday.

| Samstag | Donnerstag | Sonntag | Mittwoch | Freitag | Dienstag | Montag |

1. _____

2. _____

3. _____

4. _____

5. _____

6. _____

7. _____

B Match Column B with Column A.

A		B	
1. birthday	_____	a. Tag	
2. today	_____	b. Wochenende	
3. week	_____	c. morgen	
4. day	_____	d. Woche	
5. month	_____	e. Geburtstag	
6. school day	_____	f. Schultag	
7. tomorrow	_____	g. Monat	
8. weekend	_____	h. heute	

C Using the model, write the following dates in German.

Beispiel   Thursday, February 28 = Donnerstag, der 28. Februar

1. Saturday, June 6   _____

2. Wednesday, October 13   _____

3. Sunday, December 19   _____

4. Friday, May 21   _____

5. Tuesday, August 7   _____

D Complete each sentence with a German word.

1. If today is "Mittwoch," tomorrow is " _____."

2. If "gestern" was Saturday, " _____ " is Monday.

3. If this month is "Dezember," next month is " _____."

4. If the day before yesterday was "Donnerstag," today is

   " _____."

5. If next month is "Oktober," this month is " _____."

E Name... (*Auf deutsch, bitte.*)

1. the day when people play jokes.   _____

2. the month of Independence Day.   _____

3. the month when you send valentines.   _____

4. the day honoring the Norse goddess of love.   _____

5. the month of Halloween.   _____

F *Schreib die Wörter richtig.* Unscramble the words.

1. GEAT   _____

2. TENOAM   _____

3. UTHEE   _____

4. MADTU   _____

5. NOGANST   _____

6. IMA   _____

7. RMZÄ   _____

8. WICTHOTM   _____

9. ROMNEG   _____

10. NEAGNDORST _____

G With your classmates play "Birthday Lineup" in German. In this game all students will line up in the chronological order of their dates of birth. Begin by asking one classmate his or her birthday.

Beispiel   You say: Wann hast du Geburtstag?
             Your partner says: Ich habe am ersten August Geburtstag.

Then depending on when your birthday is, arrange yourself to the right or left of this person. You will need to ask as many classmates as possible their dates of birth in order to know if you should stand in line to the right or left of them. At the end when everyone is lined up in the correct birth order, each of you will say in turn your date of birth so that the entire class can check the accuracy of the lineup.

Was weißt du? The typical German school year starts in September and runs through June or July, depending on the area of Germany. Each of the 16 *Länder* (states) staggers its six-week summer vacation to avoid heavy congestion of Germans traveling all over the country. To the right of the annual calendar is a listing of all the holidays. Note that Germans write dates differently than we do as they announce first the day and then the month. Example: June 2 is "2. 6." Review the calendar and then write each day that is being described in German. You may need to know the meaning of these words: *Fettdruck = Sonntage und allgemeine Feiertage* (bold face = Sundays and general holidays), *Gesetzlicher Feiertag nur in bestimmten Bundesländern* (legal holiday only in designated federal states), *Weihnachtstag* (Christmas Day), *Tag der deutschen Einheit* (Day of German Unity), *Tag der Arbeit* (Labor Day), *Buß- und Bettag* (Repentance Day).

	September	Oktober	November	Dezember
Woche	35 36 37 38 39	39 40 41 42 43	44 45 46 47 48	48 49 50 51 52
Montag	6 13 20 27	4 11 18 25	1 8 15 22 29	6 13 20 27
Dienstag	7 14 21 28	5 12 19 26	2 9 16 23 30	7 14 21 28
Mittwoch	1 8 15 22 29	6 13 20 27	3 10 17 24	1 8 15 22 29
Donnerstag	2 9 16 23 30	7 14 21 28	4 11 18 25	2 9 16 23 30
Freitag	3 10 17 24	1 8 15 22 29	5 12 19 26	3 10 17 24 31
Samstag	4 11 18 25	2 9 16 23 30	6 13 20 27	4 11 18 25
Sonntag	**5 12 19 26**	**3 10 17 24 31**	**7 14 21 28**	**5 12 19 26**

	Januar	Februar	März	April
Woche	52 1 2 3 4 5	5 6 7 8 9	9 10 11 12 13	13 14 15 16 17
Montag	3 10 17 24 31	7 14 21 28	7 14 21 28	4 11 18 25
Dienstag	4 11 18 25	1 8 15 22	1 8 15 22 29	5 12 19 26
Mittwoch	5 12 19 26	2 9 16 23	2 9 16 23 30	6 13 20 27
Donnerstag	6 13 20 27	3 10 17 24	3 10 17 24 31	7 14 21 28
Freitag	7 14 21 28	4 11 18 25	4 11 18 25	1 8 15 22 29
Samstag	1 8 15 22 29	5 12 19 26	5 12 19 26	2 9 16 23 30
Sonntag	**2 9 16 23 30**	**6 13 20 27**	**6 13 20 27**	**3 10 17 24**

	Mai	Juni	Juli	August
Woche	17 18 19 20 21 22	22 23 24 25 26	26 27 28 29 30	31 32 33 34 35
Montag	2 9 16 **23** 30	6 13 20 27	4 11 18 25	1 8 15 22 29
Dienstag	3 10 17 24 31	7 14 21 28	5 12 19 26	2 9 17 23 30
Mittwoch	4 11 18 25	1 8 15 22 29	6 13 20 27	3 10 17 24 31
Donnerstag	5 **12** 19 26	2 9 16 23 30	7 14 21 28	4 11 18 25
Freitag	6 13 20 27	3 10 17 24	1 8 15 22 29	5 12 19 26
Samstag	7 14 21 28	4 11 18 25	2 9 16 23 30	6 13 20 27
Sonntag	**1 8 15 22 29**	**5 12 19 26**	**3 10 17 24 31**	**7 14 21 28**

Fettdruck = Sonntage und allgemeine Feiertage

Allgemeine Feiertage

3. 10.	Tag der deutschen Einheit
17. 11.	Buß- und Bettag
25. 12.	1. Weihnachtstag
26. 12.	2. Weihnachtstag
1. 1.	Neujahr
6. 1.	Heilige Drei Könige♣
1. 4.	Karfreitag
3. 4.	Ostersonntag
4. 4.	Ostermontag
1. 5.	Tag der Arbeit
12. 5.	Christi Himmelfahrt
22. 5.	Pfingstsonntag
23. 5.	Pfingstmontag
2. 6.	Fronleichnam♣
15. 8.	Mariä Himmelfahrt♣

♣ = Gesetzlicher Feiertag nur in bestimmten Bundesländern

1. the 18th of March: _____

2. New Year's Day: _____

3. 2. Christmas Day: _____

4. the 4th of July: _____

5. Day of German Unity: _____

6. Labor Day (in Germany): _____

7. the 30th of September: _____

8. Repentance Day: _____

9. Valentine's Day: _____

10. your birthday: _____

Unit 17

A Do you know the authors? Name the author who:

1. was a university professor as well as a dramatist.

   _____

2. is a literary critic as well as a novelist.

   _____

3. was a statesman and legal authority as well as a poet.

   _____

4. was a musician as well as a storywriter.

   _____

5. was an artist as well as a poet.

   _____

B Matching Column. Column A lists different kinds of conflicts or problems that confront literary characters. Column B lists the names of the literary works that contain these conflicts. Match Column B with Column A.

A		B
Conflicts		Works
1. imagination vs. reality _____		a. *Hebräische Balladen*
2. fulfillment vs. loss _____		b. *Der geteilte Himmel*
3. love vs. politics _____		c. *Faust*
4. knowledge vs. religion _____		d. *Wilhelm Tell*
5. love of country vs. love of family _____		e. *Nußknacker und Mäusekönig*

C A literary work may be a play, a novel, a story, a dramatic poem, a lyric poem, etc. It may appear also as a collection of poetry or stories. Can you identify each work below? Of what type of literature is each an example?

1. *Maria Stuart* _____

2. *Der siebente Tag* _____

3. *Nußknacker und Mäusekönig* _____

4. *Faust* _____

5. *Der geteilte Himmel* _____

D Name a city or geographical area associated with each author.

1. Else Lasker-Schüler _____

2. Johann Wolfgang von Goethe _____

3. Christa Wolf _____

4. Ernst Theodor Amadeus Hoffmann _____

5. Friedrich Schiller _____

E Identify the person who...

1. was a Scottish queen.

_____

2. was the artist in the famous "Blue Ride" community.

_____

3. helped a contemporary novelist decide on a literary career.

_____

4. had an influence on Charles Baudelaire and Edgar Allan Poe.

_____

5. inspired Gounod and Berlioz to write operas.

_____

Name: _____ Datum: _____

F   Kreuzworträtsel

Vertical

2. poem by Schiller
4. one of the many subjects which Goethe excelled in
5. Johann Wolfgang von....
8. In this drama Mary and Elizabeth are the main characters.
9. The opposite of romantic ideals are...ones.
11. Wilhelm Tell was a...to the Swiss freedom fighters.
12. E.T.A. Hoffmann's stories are....

Horizontal

1. famous drama by Goethe
3. E.T.A. Hoffmann used imagination and...in his stories.
6. E.T.A. Hoffmann loved this composer.
7. This symphony includes Schiller's famous poem.
10. name of a German dramatist
13. This American author was inspired by E.T.A. Hoffmann.
14. The...of freedom can be found in many classical plays.
15. This famous archer fought for Swiss freedom.
16. This city is the birthplace of Friedrich Schiller.
17. This theme can be found in Schiller's writings.

G What kind of books do you like to read? Decide if you prefer mysteries, adventure stories, science fiction or romance novels. Your teacher will designate each corner of your classroom as one of these four kinds of books. Go to the corner that represents your favorite. Pair up with a partner. Each of you tells the other why you like these books, the last book of this kind you read, its author and something about the plot. Then get together with another pair of students in your corner so that you can tell the new pair what your partner has told you. Finally, a spokesperson from each of the four groups tells the entire class something about what students from that group like to read.

H *Was weißt du?* The following 20 photos are a selection of well-known German authors from the 12th century until today. Can you identify the authors who are described?

Heinrich Böll
(1917-1985)

Wolfgang Borchert
(1921-1947)

Bert Brecht
(1898-1956)

Georg Büchner
(1813-1837)

Friedrich Dürrenmatt
(1921-1990)

Theodor Fontane
(1819-1898)

Max Frisch
(1911-1991)

Johann Wolfgang von
Goethe
(1749-1832)

Hans Jakob Christoph
von Grimmelshausen
(um 1621-1676)

Peter Handke
(1942)

Hartmann von Aue
(um 1168-um 1210)

Gerhart Hauptmann
(1862-1946)

Rolf Hochhuth
(1931)

Franz Xaver Kroetz
(1946)

Gotthold Ephraim
Lessing
(1729-1781)

*Thomas Mann
(1875-1955)*

*Friedrich von Schiller
(1759-1805)*

*Theodor Storm
(1817-1888)*

*Frank Wedekind
(1864-1918)*

*Carl Zuckmayer
(1896-1977)*

This author...

1. died in 1977:

   _____

2. was born in the 1930s and is still alive:

   _____

3. was born in 1875:

   _____

4. was only 23 or 24 years old when he died:

   _____

5. lived mostly during the 12th century:

   _____

6. was born two years before the beginning of the 20th century:

   _____

7. was the oldest among the authors shown when he died:

   _____

8. has the same first name as Storm:

   _____

9. was born last of those authors wearing glasses:

   _____

10. has three first names:

    _____

11. died at the age of 45 or 46:

    _____

12. was born one hundred years later than Theodor Storm:

    _____

Unit 18

A Select a statement from the wordbox to match the word cues.

> Ich gehe zum Fußballspiel.
>
> Ich gehe zum Strand.
>
> Ich gehe auf die Party.
>
> Ich gehe ins Museum.

1. (balloons, music and noisemakers)

   _____

2. (a soccer ball)

   _____

3. (a painting)

   _____

4. (a sand bucket, a shovel and a seashell)

   _____

B In the space provided draw a picture associated with each statement.

Beispiel   Ich lese gern.   (You draw a book.)

<u>Statement</u>   <u>Your picture</u>

1. Ich gehe zu einem Picknick.

2. Ich spiele Baseball.

3. Ich fahre gern Rad.

4. Ich gehe zum Strand.

5. Ich reite gern.

C Verbinde B mit A.

	A			B
1.	Rad	_____	a.	to dance
2.	Fußball	_____	b.	beach
3.	reiten	_____	c.	to ski
4.	spielen	_____	d.	bike
5.	tanzen	_____	e.	I
6.	Strand	_____	f.	to do, make
7.	ich	_____	g.	to play
8.	schwimmen	_____	h.	soccer
9.	Ski laufen	_____	i.	to horseback ride
10.	machen	_____	j.	to swim

D Finish each sentence with a word from the wordbox.

klar   los   Rad   Basketball   Picknick

1. Ich spiele _____ .

2. Ich fahre gern _____ .

3. Was ist da _____ ?

4. Na _____ !

5. Morgen machen wir ein _____ .

E *Was machst du gern?* Circle all the things you like to do.

1. Ich lese gern.

2. Ich schwimme gern.

3. Ich laufe gern Ski.

4. Ich spiele gern Volleyball.

5. Ich tanze gern.

6. Ich esse gern Eis.

7. Ich trinke gern Tee.

8. Ich mache gern Kreuzworträsel.

9. Ich schreibe gern.

10. Ich spreche gern am Telefon.

Name: _____ Datum: _____

F Interview five of your classmates to find out what they like to do in their free time. Ask each student the questions that follow and record each answer (*ja* or *nein*) in the space provided on this sheet.

	Student 1	Student 2	Student 3	Student 4	Student 5
1. Ich schwimme gern.	_____	_____	_____	_____	_____
2. Ich tanze gern.	_____	_____	_____	_____	_____
3. Ich lese gern.	_____	_____	_____	_____	_____
4. Ich fahre gern Rad.	_____	_____	_____	_____	_____
5. Ich reite gern.	_____	_____	_____	_____	_____
6. Ich gehe gern auf eine Party.	_____	_____	_____	_____	_____
7. Ich spiele gern Fußball.	_____	_____	_____	_____	_____
8. Ich laufe gern Ski.	_____	_____	_____	_____	_____

G Kreuzworträtsel

Vertical

1. "Ich...auch zur Party."
2. soccer game "auf deutsch" (SS=ß)
3. "Ich gehe...einem Picknick."
4. "Ich...gern."
6. "Neun weniger acht ist...."
10. "Das ist...Bleisteift."
11. "Meine Schwester ist vierzehn Jahre...."
13. "Um wieviel...beginnt die Musik?"
14. "*gehen* auf englisch"
16. "Dieter hat ein...und eine Krawatte an."
17. "Mittwoch, Donnerstag...Sonnabend"

18. "Das Wetter ist...schön. Morgen regnet es."
21. "...ist das Museum?"
23. "Julia...Käthe gehen zum Strand."
24. "Dieter und Ali spielen...."
25. "Sie sind.... Sie spielen gern Volleyball."
28. "Mein...und meine Tante kommen am Sonntag zu uns."
30. "Die... Pinakothek ist ein Museum."
33. "Welche Sportart treibst...?"
35. "Boris kommt um halb acht zur Party. ...kommt immer spät."
36. "Wieviel Uhr ist...?

Horizontal

2. unit title in German
5. "*er* auf englisch"
7. "Peter wohnt...Berlin."
8. "Die Alte Pinakothek ist ein...."
9. "Fünf...und fünf Mädchen gehen heute abend auf die Party."
12. "Was...da los?"
14. "Ich lese...ein Buch."
15. "Was...du heute?"
19. "Ich...gern."
20. "Ich...in der Ostsee."
22. "...gehe zum Fußballspiel."
25. "Martinas...kommen zu ihrer Geburtstagsparty."
26. "Ich...zwei Schwestern."
27. "*nein* auf englisch"
29. "Herr Schneider...heute einen Mantel an."
31. "Das Wetter ist heute sehr schön. Wir machen ein...am Strand."
32. "München ist eine...in Deutschland."
34. "Ich...heute Baseball."

Was weißt du? Every major German newspaper lists the results of various local, national and international sporting events. Answer the questions based on the information provided in the *Ergebnis-Telegramm* (*Results-Telegram*). You may want to know the meaning of these words: *Handball* (handball: unlike our handball, it's an indoor team sport), *Schach* (chess), *Weltmeisterschaft* (world championship), *Tischtennis* (table tennis), *Tabellenspitze* (top of the league, first place in the league), *Turnier* (tournament), *Südafrika* (South Africa).

Ergebnis-Telegramm

BASKETBALL

EM für Vereine, Männer, 2. Runde: TSV Bayer 04 Leverkusen — Canoe Jeans Den Bosch 85:60 (55:28) (Hinspiel: 83:84 - damit ist Bayer Leverkusen für die Europaliga qualifiziert).

EUROPAPOKAL der Landesmeister, Frauen, 2. Runde: BCP Ruzomberok/Slowakei — Barmer TV 67:60 (39:28) (Hinspiel: 69:92 - Barmer TV weiter).

RONCHETTI-POKAL, 2. Runde: VfL Marburg — Sparta Bertrange 81:48 (43:26) (Hinspiel: 76:51. Marburg in der 3. Runde).

2. BUNDESLIGA Süd, Frauen, 4. Spieltag: MTV Kronberg — DJK Würzburg 63:70 (34:32), KuSG Leimen — BG Bitburg/Trier 76:61 (47:27) TV Saarlouis — TSV Nördlingen 62:67 (30:30).

EISHOCKEY

NHL: New Jersey Devils — Tampa Bay Lightnings 2:1, Montreal Canadiens — Hartford Whalers 4:3, Ottawa Nordiques — Quebec Senators 5:5 n.V., Winnipeg Jets — Washington Capitals 6:4, Chicago Blackhawks — Florida Panthers 4:4 n.V., Los Angeles Kings — Vancouver Canucks 2:5, Edmonton Oilers — San Jose Sharks 3:2.

FUSSBALL

ENGLAND, Liga-Cup, 2. Runde, Rückspiele: Aston Villa — Birmingham 1:0 (Summe 2:0), Brighton — Middlesbrough 1:3 (8:1), Chelsea — West Bromwich Albion 2:1 (3:2), Derby — Exeter 2:0 (5:1), Everton — Lincoln 4:2 (8:5), Leeds — Sunderland 1:2 (4:2), Leicester — Rochdale 2:1 (8:2), Manchester United — Stoke 2:0 (3:2), Millwall — Watford 4:3 (4:3), Norwich — Bradford 3:0 (4:2), Nottingham Forest — Wrexham 3:1 (6:4), Oldham — Swansea 2:0 (3:2), Queens Park Rangers — Barnet 4:0 (6:1), Reading — Manchester City 1:2 (3:2), Sheffield Wednesday — Bolton 1:0 (2:1), Shrewsbury — Southampton 2:0 (2:1), Tottenham — Burnley 3:1 (3:1).

ITALIEN, Pokal, 2. Runde, Hinspiele: Calgiari — Cesena 1:1, Juventus Turin — Venedig 1:1, AC Mailand — Vicenza 3:0, Piacenza — Perugia 3:1, Cosenza — Atalanta Bergamo 0:2, Ascoli — AC Turin 1:3, SSC Neapel — Ancona 0:0, Lazio Rom — Avellino 0:2, Fiorentina — Reggiana 3:0, AC Parma — Palermo 2:0, Brescia — Cremonese 2:2, Foggia — Triest 2:2, Sampdoria Genua — Pisa 0:0, Udine — Lecce 2:0.

SCHOTTLAND, 10. Spieltag: Glasgow Rangers — FC Motherwell 1:2, FC St. Johnstone — Celtic Glasgow 2:1. - Die Tabellenspitze: 1. Hibernian Edinburgh 10 Spiele/15:9 Tore/13:7 Punkte, 2. FC Aberdeen 10/11:5/13:7, 3. FC Motherwell 10/13:9/13:7.

SCHWEIZ (13. Spieltag): SC Kriens — Yverdon Sports 2:0, FC Zürich — Young Boys Bern 1:2, FC Aarau — FC Sion 0:2, Xamax Neuchatel — Grasshopper Zürich 0:0, Lausanne Sport — FC Luzern 0:2. - Die Tabellenspitze: 1. Grashopper Zürich 21:8 Tore/17:7 Punkte, 2. FC Sion 16:8/15:9, 3. FC Lugano 16:12/15:9.

SPANIEN (6. Spieltag): FC Valencia — Rayo Vallecano 3:1, Celta de Vigo — Lerida 1:0, Sporting Gijon — CD Teneriffa 1:2, Real Madrid — Real Santander 2:1, FC Sevilla — Atletico Madrid 2:1, Real Sociedad San Sebastian — Real Oviedo 2:2, Albacete Balompie — Deportivo La Coruna 0:0, FC Barcelona — Real Valladolid 3:0, Real Saragossa — FC Osasuna 2:1. - Die Tabellenspitze: 1. FC Barcelona 13:2 Tore/10:2 Punkte, 2. FC Valencia 13:6/10:2, 3. Athletic Bilbao 10:4/9:1, 4. FC Sevilla 9:5/9:3.

LÄNDERSPIELE, in Los Angeles: Mexiko — Südafrika 4:0; in Brüssel: Belgien — Gabun 2:1.
KREISLIGA A Frankfurt, Gruppe Südost: Oberrad 05 Res. — TuS Makkabi 2:4.

HANDBALL

OBERLIGA, Gruppe Süd,Männer: TV Brekenheim — TuS Dotzheim 13:13, TSG Bürgel — TV Reinheim 13:18, TV Idstein — TG Hochheim 13:15, TuS Holzheim — TV Flörsheim 26:15, TV Bürgstadt — TV Wicker 20:20. - Tabellenspitze: 1. TG Hochheim 6:0 Punkte, 2. TuS Dotzheim 6:2, SG Bruchköbel.

SCHACH

PCA-WELTMEISTERSCHAFT in London, 14. Partie, Weiß Nigel Short (weiß) — Garri Kasparow (schwarz), Stand 4,5:9,5: 1. e4 c5, 2. Sf3 d6, 3. d4 cxd4, 4. Sxd4 Sf6, 5. Sc3 a6, 6. Lc4 e6, 7. Lb3 Sc6, 8. Le3 Le7, 9. f4 0-0, 10. 0-0 Sxd4, 11. Lxd4 b5, 12. e5 dxe5, 13. fxe5 Sd7, 14. Se4 Lb7, 15. Sd6 Lxd6, 16. exd6 Dg5, 17. De2 e5, 18. Lc3 Dg6, 19. Tad1 Kh8, 20. Ld5 Lxd5, 21. Txd5 De6, 22. Tfd1 Tfc8, 23. La5 Tc6, 24. b3 Tac8, 25. Lc7 Te8, 26. c4 bxc4, 27. bxc4 f5, 28. h3 h6, 29. Dc2 e4, 30. Da4 Tc5, 31. Txc5 Sxc5, 32. Dc6 Sd7, 33. Dd5 Dg6, 34. Dd2 Te5, 35. De3 De6, 36. Tc1 Tc5, 37. Tc2 Kg8, 38. a4 Kf7, 39. Df2 e3 und Remis.

TENNIS

TURNIER in Zürich (750 000 Dollar), Frauen, Einzel, 1. Runde: Navratilova (USA/Nr. 1) — Rittner (Leverkusen) 6:4, 6:1; Tauziat (Frankreich/Nr. 6) — Bollegraf (Niederlande) 4:6, 6:2, 7:6 (7:1); 2. Runde: M. Maleewa (Bulgarien/Nr. 5) — Shriver (USA) 6:0, 6:3; Oremans (Niederlande) — Wiesner (Österreich/Nr. 8) 6:2, 6:4; Maleewa-Fragniere (Schweiz/Nr. 4) — Nideffer (Südafrika) 6:2, 6:1, Cacic (Kroatien) — Neiland-Sawtschenko (Lettland) 6:3, 1:6, 6:3.

GRAND-PRIX-TURNIER in Sydney (875 000 Dollar), Männer, Einzel, 1. Runde: Borwick (Australien) — Becker (Leimen/Nr. 2) 4:6, 7:6 (8:6), 6:3; Masur (Australien/Nr. 8) — Eltingh. Achtelfinale: Korda (Tschechische Republik/Nr. 6) — Rafter (Australien) 6:4, 6:2; Ivanisevic (Kroatien/Nr. 4) — Bryan (USA) 0:6, 6:1, 6:4; Yzaga (Peru) — Masur (Australien/Nr. 8) 6:1, 6:4; Ferreira (Südafrika) — Martin (USA) 7:5, 7:6 (9:7); Woodforde (Australien) — Medwedew (Ukraine/Nr. 3) 6:2, 6:4; Canter (USA) — Borwick (Australien) 7:5, 6:3.

GRAND-PRIX-TURNIER in Toulouse (400 000 Dollar), Männer, Einzel, 1. Runde: Pioline (Frankreich/Nr. 2) — Wilander (Schweden) 7:5, 6:3. Achtelfinale: Tschesnokow (Russland) — Prinosil (Amberg) 3:6, 6:3, 6:0, Rosset (Schweiz) — Simian (Frankreich) 6:4, 6:4.

GRAND-PRIX-TURNIER in Athen (200 000 Dollar), Viertelfinale: Sanchez (Spanien/Nr. 1) — Gaudenzi (Italien/Nr. 8) 6:4, Aufgabe Gaudenzi, de la Pena (Argentinien/Nr. 7) — Schaller (Österreich) 7:6, 6:2, Arrese (Spanien) — Furlan (Italien) 6:4, 7:6, Berasategui (Spanien) — Pescosolido (Italien) 6:2, 6:2

TISCHTENNIS

EUROPALIGA, Männer, Vorrunde, Gruppe A: England — Niederlande 4:1, Polen — Schweden 4:3. - Tabelle: 1. England 4:0 Punkte/8:2 Spiele, 2. Schweden 2:2/7:5, 3. Polen 2:2/5:7, 4. Niederlande 0:4/2:8. Gruppe B: Belgien — Frankreich 4:2. - Tabelle: 1. Belgien 4:0/8:3, 2. Österreich und Deutschland 2:2/5:5, 4. Frankreich 0:4/3:8.

1. Which country won the table tennis match between England and The Netherlands?

   _____

2. In which city was the world chess championship held? _____

3. What was the final score between the handball teams TuS Holzheim vs. TV Flörsheim?

   _____

4. Who was Nigel Short's opponent in the world chess championship?

   _____

5. Which hockey team did the Edmonton Oilers beat?

   _____

6. Who is in first place in the Swiss Soccer League?

   _____

7. How much money was paid out in the tennis tournament held in Zürich, Switzerland?

   _____

8. What was the final basketball score between the women's teams MTV Kronberg vs.

   DJK Würzburg? _____ (*Note*: The halftime score is

   in parentheses.)

9. Against what country did South Africa play in soccer?

   _____

10. Who did Becker (Leimen, Germany) lose against in the first round of tennis at the

    Grand-Prix Tournament in Sydney, Australia? _____

11. How many goals did the Italian soccer team Piacenza score?

    _____

12. Which team is in first place in the handball league? _____

Unit 19

A Complete each sentence by changing the English word in parentheses to its corresponding German word.

1. (peaches)   Ich möchte vier Kilo _____ .

2. (selection)   Die _____ ist sehr groß.

3. (shopping center) Ich gehe zum _____ .

4. (expensive)   Ist das Kleid _____ ?

5. (market)   Wo ist der _____ ?

B Which item in each set of words costs more? Circle the item which probably has a more expensive price.

1. ein Lineal   ein Wintermantel

2. eine CD   ein Glas Milch

3. ein Stuhl   fünf Tomaten

4. ein Bleistift   ein Hemd

5. Tennisschuhe   ein Frühstück im Café

C A customer asks about the prices of several items. Play the part of the salesclerk as you answer each question. Make up prices that seem reasonable to you.

Beispiele Wieviel kostet die Bluse?
Die Bluse kostet DM 40,-.

Wieviel kosten die Kulis?
Die Kulis kosten DM 6,-.

1. Wieviel kostet die Jacke?

   _____

2. Wieviel kosten die Kekse?

   _____

3. Wieviel kostet eine Cola?

   _____

4. Wieviel kostet ein Basketball?

   _____

5. Wieviel kosten die Handschuhe?

   _____

D Shopping Questions. Complete the answer to each question by using a German word.

1. Was darf es sein, bitte?

   Ich _____ ein Buch kaufen.

2. Was kaufst du?

   Ich _____ Fruchtsaft.

3. Ist die CD teuer?

   Nein, sehr _____ .

4. Wo ist die Kassiererin?

   An der _____ .

5. Noch etwas?

   _____ , bitte, zehn Birnen.

E I. A quick purchase! The following is a short conversation between a salesclerk and a customer, but the sentences are all mixed up. Rearrange them by numbering them in logical sequence. Number 1 is already identified for you.

    __1__   Was darf es sein, bitte?

    _____   Nein, das ist billig.

    _____   Wieviel kostet das Eis?

    _____   Gut, ich kaufe das Eis.

    _____   Das kostet DM 2,-.

    _____   Das ist tever.

II. Now, in the space below, copy all the sentences in their correct order.

_____

_____

_____

_____

_____

_____

F Find your way to the cash register.

Which items do you pass along the way? (*Auf deutsch, bitte.*)

_____

_____

_____

_____

_____

_____

_____

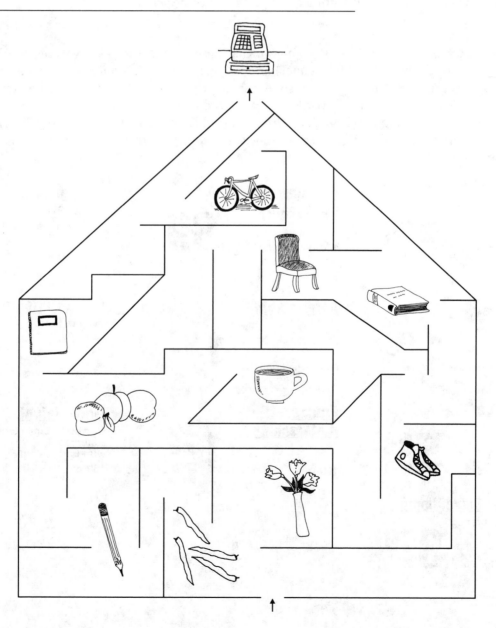

G Imagine that you're at a shopping center. You and your partner play the roles of a salesclerk and a customer. Carry on a short conversation in German in which the customer makes a purchase. Limit your questions to those you have already practiced in class and be sure to respond appropriately to your partner's questions and comments. In the course of your conversation:

1) The clerk and the customer greet each other.
2) The clerk asks the customer if he or she wants some help.
3) The customer says what he or she wants to buy and asks the price of something.
4) The clerk tells the price.
5) The customer says that he or she will buy it.
6) The clerk asks if the customer wants anything else.
7) The customer says that's all and pays for the item.
8) The clerk thanks the customer and gives him or her change.

H *Was weißt du?* When grocery shopping in Germany, it's helpful to know weights are measured in grams (1 g = 0.035 ounce) and kilos (1 kg = 2.2 pounds). Can you match the advertised groceries with their corresponding descriptions? You will not need all ten ads for your answers. Here are a few words you may need to know: *versch./verschiedene Sorten* (an assortment), *Packung* (package), *Apfelrotkohl* (red cabbage with apples), *Bienenhonig* (honey), *zarte...Würstchen* (tender...sausages, hot dogs), *Fleischwurst* (pork sausage), *Dose* (can), *Gerichte* (dishes).

Pizza
versch. Sorten

jede
320/380-g-Packung   **3.⁹⁹**

Fleischwurst
oder **Lyoner**

100-g   **-89**

3 Paar zarte Wiener Würstchen

250-g-Dose   **2.⁹⁹**

Fleischsalat oder **Geflügelsalat**

jeder 200-g-Becher   **1.⁹⁹**

Apfelrotkohl

450-g-Packung   **1.⁹⁹**

Pasta-Gerichte
versch. Sorten

jede
350-g-Packung   **2.⁹⁹**

Milupa Tee
versch. Sorten

jede 400-g-Dose   **5.⁹⁹**

Franz. Hinterschinken

100-g   **1.⁷⁹**

Lieber leicht
Cervelat-, Schinken-, Katenrauch- wurst od. Salami
100-g   **2.⁴⁹**

Langnese Bienenhonig
flüssig oder cremig

jedes 500-g-Glas   **3.⁷⁹**

1. An assortment of tea costs _____ .
2. For 2.49 marks, one can purchase _____ grams of salami.
3. A package of red cabbage weighs about _____ .
4. A jar of honey costs _____ .
5. The package that weighs a minimum of 320 grams contains an assortment of _____ .
6. The 250 gram can contains _____ .
7. The 100 grams that cost 89 pfennigs or less than one mark is for _____ .
8. The assortment of pasta dishes has a weight of _____ .

a. 350 grams
b. 3,79 marks
c. 3 pairs of tender Viennese sausages
d. 100 grams
e. pork sausage
f. 16 ounces or 1 pound
g. 5,99 marks
h. pizza

Unit 20

A What is the missing word? Can you suggest a word to complete each statement?

1. Um wieviel Uhr fährt der _____ nach Wien?

2. Hier ist der _____ .

3. Steigen Sie am Park _____ .

4. _____ steht das Flugzeug?

5. _____ Reise!

B Travel Questions. Answer each one by choosing the right letter.

1. Who carries a suitcase?

    a. ein Angestellter   b. ein Reisender

2. Which item tells you arrival and departure times?

    a. ein Fahrplan   b. eine Fahrkarte

3. Which item permits you to travel internationally?

    a. ein Reisepaß   b. eine Karte

4. How can you get to Leipzig?

    a. mit dem Bleistift   b. mit dem Zug

5. Which words tell you where something is?

    a. dort drüben, links   b. um acht Uhr

C   **I. Give the German name for a vehicle associated with each word below.**

     1.   Flughafen _____

     2.   Bahnhof   _____

     3.   Ozean   _____

     4.   Straße   _____

   II. Now write in German that you are traveling (or riding) in each of these vehicles.

     1. _____

     2. _____

     3. _____

     4. _____

D   Connect the answers in Column B to their corresponding questions.

	A			**B**
1.	Wo ist der Flugsteig?	_____	a.	am Park
2.	Wo steige ich aus?	_____	b.	um 9.30
3.	Hast du eine Fahrkarte?	_____	c.	im Koffer
4.	Um wieviel Uhr fährt der Bus?	_____	d.	dort drüben, rechts
5.	Wo ist der Reisepaß?	_____	e.	ja

E   Fill in each sentence with a word from the wordbox.

Koffer   Fahrkarte   Uhr   Bahnhof   Reisepaß

     1.   Ich fahre mit dem Taxi zum _____ .

     2.   Ich fahre um 10 _____ nach Berlin.

     3.   Ich habe einen _____ und einen

         _____ .

     4.   Ich kaufe eine _____ am Schalter.

F *Was weißt du?* Germans love to travel around Germany and to other countries in the world. Therefore, it's not surprising to find numerous travel ads in daily German newspapers. Can you find the answers in the travel ads? Here are some words that will help you in your answers: *die größte der Nordfriesischen Inseln* (the largest of the North Frisian islands), *Tg.* (abbreviation for *Tag* or *Tage*), *mit Inselrundfahrt...Ostseekreuzfahrt* (with trip around island...Baltic Sea cruise).

1. The *R.o.l.a.n.d.-Reisen* travel agency is located in the city of

    _____ .

2. The name of the largest North Frisian island is

    _____ .

3. A one-day trip to Dresden (except on Saturdays) costs

    _____ marks.

4. It costs 149 marks to go on a two-and-a-half-day trip to Prag, Breslau or to

    _____ .

5. A ten-day trip to Spain costs _____ marks.

6. The travel special that costs 269 marks for a four-day trip is to

    _____ .

7. The price of 219 marks is for a two-and-a-half-day trip to

    _____ .

8. It costs 169 marks to go on a trip to Vienna (Wien) and

    _____ .

9. The cost for a one-day cruise around the island of Usedom including a Baltic Sea cruise

    is _____ marks.

10. The complete price for a round-trip to Breslau is

    _____ marks.

11. Those who are interested in any of the listed trips can call the travel agency at (phone

    number) _____ .

12. The *Heidepark* is located in _____ .

Name: _____ Datum: _____

 Unscramble the words.

1. FISHFC _____

2. GULFEGUZ _____

3. UGZ _____

4. TOLHE _____

5. HRAKATFER _____

6. HANFHOB _____

7. ISEER _____

8. SBU _____

9. FKFROE _____

10. EERSISAPS (SS=ß) _____

H Imagine that you're in a German train station. You and your partner play the roles of a clerk at the ticket counter and a traveler. Carry on a short conversation in German in which the traveler buys a train ticket. Limit your questions to those you have already practiced in class and be sure to respond appropriately to your partner's questions and comments. In the course of your conversation:

1) The clerk and the traveler greet each other.
2) The traveler tells the clerk what city he or she is going to and asks at what time the next train for that city is leaving.
3) The clerk tells the traveler the time.
4) The traveler tells the clerk that he or she wants a round-trip ticket in second class and asks the price.
5) The clerk tells the traveler the price.
6) The traveler pays for the ticket.
7) The clerk thanks the traveler and gives him or her change.